Catholicism and Buddhism

Catholicism and Buddhism

The Contrasting Lives and Teachings
of Jesus and Buddha

by ANTHONY E. CLARK

Foreword by CARL E. OLSON

CASCADE *Books* · Eugene, Oregon

CATHOLICISM AND BUDDHISM
The Contrasting Lives and Teachings of Jesus and Buddha

Cascade Books
An Imprint of Wipf and Stock Publishers
199 W. 8th Ave., Suite 3
Eugene, OR 97401

www.wipfandstock.com

PAPERBACK ISBN: 978-1-5326-1818-5
HARDCOVER ISBN: 978-1-4982-4353-7
EBOOK ISBN: 978-1-4982-4352-0

Cataloguing-in-Publication data:

Names: Clark, Anthony E., author. | Olson, Carl E., foreword.

Title: Catholicism and Buddhism : the contrastings lives and teachings of Jesus and Buddha / Anthony E. Clark.

Description: Eugene, OR: Cascade Books, 2018 | Includes bibliographical references and index.

Identifiers: ISBN 978-1-5326-1818-5 (paperback) | ISBN 978-1-4982-4353-7 (hardcover) | ISBN 978-1-4982-4352-0 (ebook)

Subjects: LCSH: Christianity and other religions—Buddhism. | Buddhism—Relations— Christianity.

Classification: BV4905.3 .C9 .C45 2018 (paperback) | BV4905.3 (ebook)

Manufactured in the U.S.A.   03/30/18

Contents

Foreword
by Carl E. Olson

ABOUT FIFTEEN YEARS AGO, while browsing in a large bookstore (part of a now defunct national chain), I was suddenly struck by a strange sense of disproportion. As I stood in the middle of the large "Religion" section, I noticed how one entire, long wall of books was devoted to Eastern religions, the majority of them about Buddhism: the history of Buddhism, the story of the Buddha, and how to practice various types of Buddhism, especially Zen Buddhism. If someone guessed the religious demographics of the local population, based only on the books in the store—with titles such as *Jesus and Buddha: The Parallel Sayings* and *Going Home: Jesus and Buddha as Brothers*—they might conclude that a quarter or a third are Buddhists of some sort, with another large chunk being Christian, and a notable number either atheists or practitioners of some strain of Western esotericism, often lumped together as the "New Age movement."

Self-identifying Buddhists, however, make up a very small percentage of the population in the United States. Recent data from PRRI's American Values Atlas, which uses data gathered from 50,000 annual telephone interviews, indicates that about 1 percent of Americans identify as Buddhist, with the highest numbers found in Hawaii (4 percent), California (2 percent), and Delaware (2 percent). Buddhism has fewer adherents in the fifty states than Islam, the Latter-day Saints (Mormonism), The Watchtower Society (Jehovah's Witnesses), or Eastern Orthodoxy—yet it appears in many ways to have a more substantial cultural footprint. Put another way, the bookstore I visited—and it was quite similar to many others, big and small—did not have a noticeable section promoting the joy of being a Jehovah's Witness or the spiritual insights of Mormonism.

Why, then, so much interest in Buddhism, and why so many recent books on the topic? There are, of course, several reasons, as my good friend Dr. Anthony E. Clark discusses in this welcome, helpful, and timely book— a book that had its origins in an article Tony and I co-authored in 2005. Tony and I first met around the same time I had my modest epiphany in the bookstore; he was finishing his doctorate in Chinese history at the University of Oregon and I had co-authored a book, *The Da Vinci Hoax*, about the massive popularity of Dan Brown's mega-selling novel. That novel, *The Da Vinci Code*, was successful in large part because it subverted, however crudely and inaccurately, Christian history and belief while drawing upon various strands of esoteric belief systems and gnostic-fueled conspiracy theories. Over the course of several conversations, Tony and I discussed our shared belief that the same "spiritual but not religious" movement, which helped sell over 80 million copies of Brown's novel, was also part of the continued, swelling interest in Buddhism and other Eastern belief systems. A perfect example of this can be found in the 1997 best-selling book *Living Buddha, Living Christ* by prolific Buddhist monk and author Thich Nhat Hanh, which includes a glowing introduction by Elaine Pagels, a Princeton scholar known for popular books such as *The Gnostic Gospels* (1979) and *Beyond Belief* (2003).

The essay on Catholicism and Buddhism that Tony and I wrote for *This Rock* magazine (now *Catholic Answers Magazine*) was meant to help Catholics understand the appeal of Buddhism and to recognize the points of agreement and disagreement between the two traditions. We noted that Buddhism attracts Westerners, including more than a few Christians, because so many in the West desire spiritual vitality in the midst of the emptiness of secular life and long for inner peace in a world bursting with chaos and conflict. In addition, Buddhism has an apparently non-dogmatic and open-minded character; it attracts those eager to move beyond what they view as the rigid rules and outdated perspectives of orthodox Christianity.

But, as we noted in that essay, and as Tony discusses with far more detail in the book you are holding, for every person who embraces Buddhism completely, there are numerous others who pick and choose from Buddhism according to their particular appetites and circumstances. (One notable example of this can be found in the growing "mindfulness" movement, which in many cases has taken a practice and characteristic of

Buddhist meditation and turned it into a form of new spirituality that is to Buddhism what Taco Bell menus are to authentic Mexican cuisine.) While Buddhism can be learned and practiced in a systematic, comprehensive way, most Americans encounter and receive it in bits, pieces, and fragments, often through the vehicles of popular movies and television shows.

This is because, frankly, Americans have a certain genius (if that's the right word) for syncretism and the individualistic customization of beliefs related to "faith" and "spirituality." In the Catholic Church there is sometimes reference made to "cafeteria Catholicism," as when a Catholic embraces many of the Church's teachings on peace and justice but ignore or even reject teachings about sexuality and marriage. The irony is that more than a few "cafeteria Catholics" end up practicing—or dipping into and dabbling within—what I call "buffet Buddhism." Consequently, they are partially and imperfectly catechized in both Catholicism and Buddhism.

And that is why this book, meant for a popular audience but rooted in a wealth of scholarship and personal experience, is so important. Tony, a life-long Catholic, has been studying Asian culture and thought since he was a young boy growing up on the Oregon coast. Having spent time in China and Taiwan while earning a doctorate in Chinese literature and history from the University of Oregon, Tony subsequently lived in Beijing and Taipei while writing books on Catholicism in China. He has spent long stretches of time visiting Buddhist monasteries and has studied Buddhism directly, both as a scholar and as someone who counts many practicing Buddhists as good friends. Tony has also studied theology, liturgy, and Church history as a seminarian for the diaconate in the Byzantine Catholic Church—and so he is well-versed in Eastern Christianity as well as Eastern religions including Buddhism and Hinduism. In sum, he brings a most unique combination of gifts to this volume, not least the sort of charitable, thoughtful perspective befitting his vocation as a highly regarded professor and educator.

While Tony's beliefs as a serious and practicing Catholic are evident, this book never falls into the trap of triumphalist hubris and avoids the quicksand of syncretism. The result is a work that is charitable and clear-eyed, nuanced and direct, detailed and accessible. When Tony first began working on this book, we discussed the goal and audience. Tony's goal, drawing on the encouragement of Fr. Mitch Pacwa, SJ, was to reach and assist a wide, non-specialist readership. That is one reason he decided to employ a Q&A format, the better to help readers approach and digest an often daunting and complex topic. In doing so, he has moved well past both "cafeteria Catholicism" and "buffet Buddhism," which are both weak pretenders to the real things, and has presented a full course meal consisting of theological and philosophical discussion, robust interreligious dialogue, and personal reflection.

Carl E. Olson, MTS
2 May 2017
The Feast of St. Athanasius, Patron of Theologians

Acknowledgments

Meister Eckhart once said that, "If the only expression you uttered in your whole life was 'thank you,' that would suffice," though it would take a whole lifetime to sufficiently thank those whose help and support made this book possible. First I offer my deepest gratitude to my friends and intellectual colleagues, Carl E. Olson and Eric Cunningham. Carl was largely the inspiration for this book and proposed several of the questions, and Eric rendered helpful comments as it approached its final form; Carl's trenchant insight into the theological distinctions between Catholic Christianity and Buddhism, and Eric's incisive apprehension of the historical differences between the two are discerned throughout what I have written here. In many ways, they have served as wise *muni*, or "sages," that have helped clarify several spiritual points of view, Christian and Buddhist, that I have struggled to reconcile over the past decade. As I penned this book in several locations—at home in Washington State or in Asia—I benefitted from the generous support of kind persons, institutions, and granting agencies.

I render my warmest thanks for the support of the National Endowment for the Humanities/American Council for Learned Societies, the Chiang Ching-Kuo Foundation, the William J. Fulbright Foundation, the National Security Education Program, the Congregation of the Mission Vincentian Studies Institute (DePaul University), and the Weyerhaeuser Center for Christian Faith & Learning, directed by my friend and colleague Dale Soden. Wu Yinghui of Minzu University of China kindly provided me housing at Minzu while working on this and another project; his generosity provided a congenial space to live and write, surrounded by tousled piles of paper and stacks of books. I also thank my colleagues at Whitworth University, especially my friends in the Department of History, whose continuous support and encouragement continue to make life and work at Whitworth a constant pleasure. Tibo Colman, one of my research assistants as the Lindaman Endowed Chair, offered valuable feedback and editorial assistance as I finalized a draft of this book, and for his insight I am deeply thankful.

In my effort to understand the multileveled and often opaque nuances of Buddhist belief and Christian doctrine I have benefitted from the privilege of several encounters with other scholars and thinkers who have similarly engaged the conundrum of religious and cultural exchange. I recall with fondness dialogues with Stephen Durrant, Matthew Wells, He Jianjun, Lionel Jensen, Wendy Larson, Father William O'Brien, and especially Kyoko Tokuno, with whom I studied Buddhist history and belief while an inquisitive student at the University of Oregon. Professor Tokuno once delivered a lecture on the Buddhist understanding of time and impermanence while sitting in the lotus position on a table in front of the class. I also had enlightening (no pun intended) dialogues with Mark Unno, also a specialist on Buddhism at the University of Oregon, on the relative meanings and applications of the Buddhist Dharma in the modern world. It is also important, I believe, to thank an anonymous Buddhist nun I once met at a temple in Taipei, who saw me approaching the front gate and welcomed me with the salutation: "Welcome. You're a Catholic, are you not?" We had a delightful discussion about the differences between Catholicism and Buddhism, and I still do not know how she knew I am a Catholic. The message I discerned from her was that a straightforward and accurate comparison of these two traditions was necessary, one that does not seek to falsely ascribe similarities where they do not exist and seek reconciliation where it is already present. Her thoughts have been present throughout the writing of this work.

Finally, I thank my wife, Amanda, a distinguished scholar herself, for her enduring support and help as I thought and wrote about two spiritual traditions that have held my interest for nearly two decades. To her this book is dedicated.

Are Jesus and Buddha "Brothers"?

I am accustomed to writing dispassionate academic works based on sustained research and scholarly collaboration. This book is something entirely new for me; it represents many years of informed musings from the view of a Catholic Christian. This is not what I would call "scholarship," but rather a scholar's engagement with another, and deeply admired, religious tradition. I hope my readers do not become mired in particular assertions made throughout what follows, but suspend their conclusions about what I am suggesting until having completed the final page.

This book emerged mainly from exchanges I have had with several bright students who have enrolled in my courses on the history of Buddhism. They have frequently remarked: "Professor Clark, you speak so often about the merits of Buddhism, but you're a Christian. If you were asked to clearly provide distinctions that separate Christianity from Buddhism, what questions would you address and what differences would you highlight?" What follows here is an attempt to respond to these students, most of whom are Christians themselves seeking to better understand how Christianity and Buddhism are not the same. What follows consists largely of reflections from my own point of view as a Catholic, reflections intended to incite more dialogue between these two important spiritual traditions. My intention is not to be pugnacious, but rather to avoid intellectual evasion for the sake harmony between Buddhists and Christians. I wish rather to render an honest representation of what the core of Buddhism and Catholicism teaches and believes. At the end of the day, I am, however, more comfortable with nuance and complexity than the following pages might suggest. That said, differences remain, and this book does not represent the first attempt to untangle the contrasting lives and teachings of Jesus and the Buddha.

In 1929, G. K. Chesterton was already confronting the same misconceptions about Christianity and Buddhism that we face today. Chesterton lamented a prevailing religious view that, as he put it: "Buddhism is Christianity, and Buddhism is better than Christianity, and Christianity will never be itself until it is enlightened enough to become something different."[1] This remark was made after he had read an announcement in a newspaper that an unnamed Chinese Buddhist would soon visit London, who, as an enlightened Easterner, would be "finally abolishing war." The announcement compared the "enlightened condition of Buddhists" with "the benighted condition of Christians."[2] Western, Christian society had just begun to recover from the First World War, and like today, Christianity was popularly blamed for its "inability" to prevent human violence. And so, the secular media pundits began to suggest the "failure" of Christianity, and many recommended that Christendom should be supplemented, perhaps even saved or replaced by Buddhism. Chesterton was not deceived by such sophistry, however, for the Buddhist cultures of the East were no less violent and antagonized than the Christian cultures of the West. China's furious civil war, made even worse by the fierce invasion by Japan, was a case in point during Chesterton's lifetime.

"Fighting," Chesterton said, "has never been a habit strictly confined to Christians, nor have wars been entirely unknown outside Christendom."[3] The Western discontent with Christianity was less about what Christianity teaches, he suggested, than with how selfish and ungodly people behave when they do not truly follow those teachings. "It is no disgrace to Christianity," Chesterton continued, "it is no disgrace to any religion, that its counsels of perfection have not made every single person perfect."[4] It is not my point here to suggest that Buddhism does not offer good and useful suggestions for how to better behave and get along in our damaged world. It is not that Buddhism and Christianity have not offered reasonable recommendations for avoiding war, it is that their recommendations have been largely ignored. More to the point of this book, however, is my aim to help Christians become better aware that Buddhism and Christianity are not

1. Chesterton, "Buddhism and Christianity."
2. Ibid.
3. Ibid.
4. Ibid.

the same. And furthermore, I suggest that the assumption that Christianity is somehow improved when supplemented by Buddhism is to imply that Christ, who is the Divine founder of Christianity, has failed to leave his Church the sufficient and effective means for peace and personal salvation. In his final words in response to the coming Chinese Buddhist who would at last abolish all wars during his visit to London, Chesterton directs criticism away from the teachings of Christ, and condemns, "the muddled discontent of worldly people, who curse the Church for not saving the world that did not want to be saved."[5]

Contending Voices

We see today many Christians, including Catholic Christians, who unwittingly accept the popular notion that Christianity is better practiced as a "Christian Buddhist" or "Buddhist Christian," as if Buddhism is somehow more "peaceful" or "informed" than what was taught by Jesus and handed down by his disciples. If we let Christ speak for himself, such an assertion appears outlandish. In the gospel of Matthew, for example, Jesus directed his followers to, "Love your neighbor as yourself," but unlike Buddhism, which has no belief in a personal and omnipotent God, Jesus places loving one's neighbor after the command to, "Love the Lord your God with all your heart and with all your soul and with all your mind" (Matt 22: 34-40). And in his most famous sermon Jesus announced on the Mount that, "Blessed are the peacemakers, for they will be called the children of God" (Matt 5:9). The Buddha also taught of peace: "He is a sage who has abandoned violence towards living beings," he said, "be they moving or stationary, and who neither kills nor causes others to kill."[6] In another quote, the Buddha told his followers that, "Peace comes from within. Do not seek it without."[7] The important distinction between the teachings of Christianity and Buddhism is that in Christianity peace only reaches perfection when it is understood and practiced within the context of belief in the One God who is revealed to us in Scripture. Some Christians today harbor the belief that Buddhism can improve, or even correct, the teachings of Christ and the Church. For some, remaining a Christian rests on the belief that Jesus and the Buddha

---

5. Ibid.

6. See Wallis, *Dhammapada*, Verse 405.

7. Quoted in Alen, *The Buddha's Philosophy*, 63.

be viewed as "brothers" who compliment and complete each other, as if there are no contradictions between their teachings.

Recent decades have seen an increasing number of books comparing Jesus to Buddha, and at times these works suggest that Christianity and Buddhism are best practiced together. The professor of theology at Union Theological Seminary, Paul F. Knitter, published his popular book, *Without Buddha I Could Not be a Christian*, which, among other creative theological assumptions, argues for a kind of "double belonging," wherein one can draw from more than one religious tradition for spiritual belief and solace.[8] When asked in an interview with the *National Catholic Reporter* what he means by "double belonging," Knitter responded that, "more and more people are finding that they can be genuinely nourished by more than one religious tradition, by more than their home tradition or their native tradition."[9] Being "nourished" by more than one religious tradition, according to Knitter's theology, largely implies the intermixing of these traditions; Buddhism and Christianity appear to melt together into one, new religious soup, even if his book attempts to retain a Christian identity by making Buddhism an "adjective" and Christianity a "noun." In his interview Knitter declares that, "So for me now when I say the word God, what I image, what I feel, thanks to Buddhism, is the interconnecting spirit—this ever-present spirit, this ever-present, interconnecting energy that is not a person, but is very personal."[10] This intermixing is problematic, as "thanks to Buddhism," according to Knitter's understanding of God, the God who became Man for man's salvation, has become an "interconnecting energy" that is less understandable in biblical than in popular relativistic terms.

Another Catholic who affirms that her Christian faith is "enriched by Buddhism" is Susan J. Stabile, a professor of Law at the University of St. Thomas. In an essay she wrote for the *Huffington Post*, Stabile asserts that, "But for Buddhism, I could not be Catholic today."[11] It is her own sense of "independence and self-sufficiency," she suggests, that triggered her former turn away from Catholicism, but "Buddhism's individuality was much more consonant with my self-image, and Buddhism offered me a means of developing a spirituality that facilitated my eventual return to God."[12] She writes

8. See Knitter, *Without Buddha I Could Not Be a Christian*.

9. Fox, "Double belonging: Buddhism and Christian faith."

10. Ibid.

11. Stabile, "A Christian Faith Enriched by Buddhism."

12. Ibid.

that, "The Buddhist concept of emptiness gave me a way of understanding the Christian notion on dying to self and rising in Christ. The Buddhist understanding of impermanence helps me deal with difficult mental states and feelings."[13] Like Knitter, Stabile suggests that Scripture, the Church, and Tradition are incomplete avenues to God; they are supplemented by Buddhism for their fulfillment. In her book, *Growing in Love and Wisdom: Tibetan Buddhist Sources for Christian Meditation*, she suggests that Tibetan Buddhism is an effective and helpful aid for Christian prayer and contemplation, and compares Saint Ignatius of Loyola's *Spiritual Exercises* to Tibetan meditation techniques.[14] Concluding her essay for the *Huffington Post*, Stabile exclaims, "Perhaps the greatest influences Buddhism has had on my Catholicism is my openness to different ways of being Catholic."[15] What is meant by "different ways of being Catholic" requires clarification, because the Church has always insisted that even with its apparent wide doctrinal boundaries, there remain limits to what one may believe and remain a Catholic Christian. While it may be historically true that Christianity has learned from and transformed what other religions have taught, it has not been essentially changed by or become part of those religious traditions.

It is doubtful that G. K. Chesterton could have imagined how accepted and widespread the turn toward Buddhism has become in the twenty-first century among Catholics and Catholic institutions. The Jesuit priest, Father Robert E. Kennedy, SJ, identifies himself as a "Roshi," Zen Master, and conducts Buddhist retreats at his Morning Star Zendo in Jersey City, and at the Ignatian Center for Jesuit Education at the Catholic Santa Clara University, "Zen meditation and mindfulness sitting practice" is held every week. Far more difficult is it to find opportunities for the Holy Rosary, the Benedictine practice of Lectio Divina, or the Spiritual Exercises of Saint Ignatius, whose namesake they both claim. Catholic retreat centers, such as the Renewal Center operated by the Redemptorist Fathers, commonly sponsor Zen Buddhist practices on their events calendars. Whether or not one can be both a Buddhist and a Christian, and whether books like Marcus Borg's *Jesus and Buddha: The Parallel Sayings* reliably represent what Christ taught, are among the principal questions confronted by this book. Within the Church there are many contending voices regarding the role Buddhism has in or out of Christianity, and whether the Church's long

13. Ibid.

14. Stabile, *Growing in Love and Wisdom*, 72.

15. Stabile, "A Christian Faith Enriched by Buddhism."

history of prayer, meditation, philosophy, theology, and aesthetic expression can be, or should be, supplemented with the teachings of the Buddha.

As a starting point to meeting these important questions I believe that God and his Church already provide reliable and authoritative answers, and on the question of Buddhism the Church has not been silent. In its statement, "Christ and the Other Religions," the Church's Commission for Interreligious Dialogue speaks clearly on the centrality of the God question when considering Buddhism in light of Christian belief. "Since Buddha deliberately avoided talking about the existence or non-existence of God," the document states, "it is obvious that Buddhists will have difficulty when faced with the Christian belief in Jesus as the Son of God, true God and true man."[16] Despite the real or imagined similarities between Catholicism and Buddhism, the Commission asserts, there remains, "a fundamental difference, for they accept Jesus as a wise Teacher, but not as a divine Person."[17]

The Approach

As a believing and practicing Catholic, my approach to the subject of Christian and Buddhist comparison is admittedly one-sided, since I believe that Jesus Christ is who he said he is. When Saint Thomas asked Jesus, "How can we know the way?" Jesus answered, "I am the way the truth and the life," and just before this he said, "Do not let your hearts be troubled. You believe in God; believe also in me" (John 14:1). Catholics accept the Church's role as the arbiter of God's voice through the Magisterium, and also accept that the Truth that is found only in Jesus Christ and the Church is the foundation upon which dialogue properly begins. In his homily before the conclave that selected Pope Benedict XVI, then Cardinal Joseph Ratzinger, used the term "dictatorship of relativism" to describe one of the intellectual and spiritual afflictions of our time. "Today, having a clear faith based on the Creed of the Church is often labeled as fundamentalism," he said in his homily; this is a "dictatorship of relativism that does not recognize anything as definitive and whose ultimate goal consists solely of one's own ego and desires."[18] Cardinal Ratzinger also explained in his homily that the Church, as bearer of the truth, offers the world nothing less than friendship with

16. "Christ and the Other Religions," Commission for Interreligious Dialogue, draft written by Michael Fizgerald.

17. Ibid.

18. Ratzinger, Pre-Conclave Homily.

Christ himself. "It is this friendship that opens us up to all that is good and gives us a criterion by which to distinguish the true from the false, and deceit from truth."[19]

Catholicism believes in the singular divinity of the One God and in the immutability of the truth given to the Church by Christ, and thus it inevitably encounters friction when communicating that claim to members of other, or no faith traditions, despite its best attempts to soften its message with charity. That said, while I believe in the claims and faith of Catholicism, I hold many of the practices of Buddhists in high esteem, and I recommend reading Pope Paul VI's "Declaration on the Church's Relation to Non-Christian Religions," *Nostra Aetate* to anyone who wishes to understand the Church's view of other faith traditions. In this proclamation, Pope Paul VI, affirmed that:

> The Catholic Church rejects nothing that is true and holy in these religions. She regards with sincere reverence those ways of conduct and of life, those precepts and teachings which, though differing in many aspects from the ones she holds and sets forth, nonetheless often reflect a ray of that Truth which enlightens all men.[20]

This statement is directly followed, however, with an affirmation of the Church's continued duty to confirm the Catholic faith to all persons: "Indeed, she proclaims, and ever must proclaim Christ 'the way, the truth, and the life' (John 14:6), in whom men may find the fullness of religious life, in whom God has reconciled all things to Himself."[21]

The differing notions of truth and dialogue sometimes create challenges when Catholics and Buddhists engage in authentic dialogue. The popular Vietnamese Zen Buddhist, Thic Nhat Hanh, has eloquently said that, "In true dialogue, both sides are willing to change," but as attractive as his suggestion is, the Catholic is not at liberty to change what God, the creator of all things, has said. Catholics, such as I, the author of this book, who retain a "stubborn attachment to the catechism," are often reminded by more "open-minded" interlocutors that, "Real dialogue is not two monologues." The answer to this accusation is somewhat paradoxical; liberty is only known within the confines of God's unchanging truth. When Thomas Merton entered the Trappist monastery at Gethsemane, Kentucky—the Order of Cistercians of the Strict Observance—he wrote that the Brother,

19. Ibid.

20. *Nostra Aetate*, 2.

21. Ibid.

"locked the gate behind me and I was enclosed in the four walls of my new freedom."[22]

As appealing, and seemingly peace-facilitating, as it seems to view religious difference pluralistically, assigning equal value and truthfulness to all religious paths, this is not what the Church teaches, and it is not what Christ himself taught. In his encyclical letter, "Charity in Truth," *Caritas Veritate*, Pope Benedict XVI outlined well how I envisioned the approach of this book in light of what Christ has imparted:

> Only in truth does charity shine forth, only in truth can charity be authentically lived. Truth is the light that gives meaning and value to charity. That light is both the light of reason and the light of faith, through which the intellect attains to the natural and super-natural truth of charity: it grasps its meaning as gift, acceptance, and communion. Without truth, charity degenerates into senti-mentality. Love becomes an empty shell, to be filled in an arbitrary way. In a culture without truth, this is the fatal risk facing love. It falls prey to contingent subjective emotions and opinions, the word "love" is abused and distorted, to the point where it comes to mean the opposite.[23]

With this in mind, I have attempted to speak charitably and truthfully about the similarities and differences between Catholicism and Buddhism, and it is my hope that this book will help Catholics, and our Buddhist friends to better understand the Catholic faith as it is distinguished from Buddhism.

As for organization, I have arranged this book as a dialogue, which begins with a question and is followed first by a Buddhist explanation and second by a Catholic response. Catholics will readily notice the use of the traditional catechism format. I hope that this system not only allows the reader to better recognize the important distinctions between Catholicism and Buddhism, but may along the way help the reader acquire a deeper appreciation for the teachings of Christ and the Catholic faith. I represent two distinct perspectives: as a historian of Asia and a scholar of religious comparisons. Those with advanced training in Catholic and Buddhist belief might find some of my explanations over-simplistic and under-nuanced. I readily admit that this book is intended as an introduction and not an exhaustive scholarly treatise, and I also respond with an astute comment

22. Thomas Merton, *The Seven Story Mountain* (New York: Harcourt, Brace and Company, 1948), 372.

23. Benedict XVI, *Caritas in Veritate*, 3.

by the Harvard professor of philosophy, George Santayana, who said that, "The spirit's foe in man has not been simplicity, but sophistication." Sometimes the more "sophisticated" language of scholars muddies the waters of clarity, and does little good for a world seeking truth.

Jesus and Buddha: The Parallels

Jack Kornfield, in his introduction to Marcus Borg's *Jesus and Buddha: The Parallel Sayings*, recounts visiting a Buddhist monastery in the Mekong Delta of Vietnam. He visited the island monastery during active fighting, and after the monks had greeted him on the shore they took him:

> . . . to the end of the island where, on the top of a hill, there was an enormous fifty-foot tall statue of a standing Buddha. Next to Buddha stood an equally tall statue of Jesus. They had their arms around each others' shoulders, smiling. While helicopter gunships flew overhead and the war raged around us, Buddha and Jesus stood there like brothers, expressing compassion and healing for all who would follow their way.[24]

This is indeed a moving story, and it may be that Jesus would embrace the Buddha as a fellow man of peace, but are they really like brothers? And can we truthfully say that Jesus would have recommended "their way," as if both paths are equal? Jesus identified himself as God and left the Church and divine revelation to guide us to salvation. The Buddha identified himself neither as a god nor as man, per se, and told his followers to work out their salvation on their own. He believed himself to be a reincarnated being, a manifestation of the fleeting reality, or unreality, of impermanence. According to the Buddhist scriptures, "The last words of the Tathagata (one who has thus gone) were: 'Behold, O monks, this is my last advice to you. All component things in the world are impermanent. They are not lasting. Work hard to gain your own salvation.'"[25] From the Catholic point of view, the "brotherhood" of Jesus and Buddha exists inasmuch as Jesus was made Incarnate as a human being, and that the historic Buddha, as Siddhartha Gautama, an Indian noble, was also a human being. Their symbolic brotherhood was limited to this shared humanity; the Buddha was not, as Jesus is, God, part of the Holy Trinity. Their teachings might remarkably overlap

24. Kornfield, "Introduction," ii.

25. The Buddha, "Maha-Parinirvana Sutra," Part 6: 8. Also see E. H. Brewster, *The Life of Gotama the Buddha*, 225.

at times, but as the Catholic Church teaches, only faith in Christ and the sacraments of the Church can bring a person into the fullness of truth and peace.

The notion of "many paths to the same end" is more a Buddhist idea than a Christian one. In an interview the Dalai Lama stated that, "According to different religious traditions, there are different methods. For example, a Christian practitioner may meditate on God's grace, God's infinite love. This is a very powerful concept in order to achieve peace of mind. A Buddhist practitioner may be thinking about relative nature and also Buddha-nature. This is also very useful."[26] Christianity and Buddhism, Jesus and Buddha, he suggests, may be equally effective ways to the same goal. In an online Christian discussion forum, one reader stated that, "Buddha was just a philosopher who urged men to be selfless. Jesus was just a philosopher who urged men to be selfless. Love is just another word for selfless."[27] Jesus was "just a philosopher"? Buddhists might answer yes, and Christians should answer no. Convenient parallels between Christ and the Buddha are misleading and often misrepresent the teachings of the Catholic Church. Buddhism, the fourth largest religious tradition in the world, has around 370 million followers. And while less than one percent of Americans identify themselves as Buddhists, many popular bookstores often carry an equal or greater number of books about Buddhism than Christianity; works by the Dalai Lama are often seen beside those of the Pope or Mother Teresa, hinting at their "similarities." Buddhism is sometimes seen as "a more acceptable" religious option, as it is thought to be a more favorable path to understanding and peace, and perhaps even an equally effective path to salvation as the one outlined by Jesus.

The appeal for peace, it seems, is the most common attraction to Buddhism among Christians and non-Christians, as if peace is better attained, or expressed, through the Buddhist tradition than it is in Christianity. The reader has already seen above how Chesterton has confronted this claim. Human persons cannot help but lament world violence and experience anxiety in a world so determined on change and novelty. The Church for her part accepts the efforts Buddhism makes to attain peace, and in *Nostra Aetate*, Pope Paul VI affirmed: "Buddhism, in its various forms, realizes the radical insufficiency of this changeable world."[28] The goal in this book

26. Harris, "The Peaceful Mind."
27. Christian Discussion Forum, "Buddha vs. Jesus."
28. *Nostra Aetate*, 2.

is to point Catholics, and non-Catholics, toward the fullness of peace and truth, which is sufficiently offered in the Church founded by Jesus Christ. And despite the popular appeals made to Buddhism for an answer to world violence and human apathy, and as some turn away from Christianity and its "outdated teachings," I suggest that even with Buddhism's salutary message of world harmony, true peace is best found in the God of Christianity. As Thomas Merton once wrote, "We are not at peace with others because we are not at peace with ourselves, and we are not at peace with ourselves because we are not at peace with God."[29]

29. Thomas Merton, *The Living Bread*, 157.

SECTION ONE

History and Context

Q: Who was the Buddha? Who was Jesus?

The story of the historic Buddha is very unlike the life of the historic Jesus of Nazareth. Buddhism derives from the teachings of the sixth-century BC Indian nobleman, or prince, Siddhartha Gautama, who later became the Buddha, which means, "the awakened one." The dominant religion around him was Brahmanism, the historic predecessor to Hinduism, which teaches such doctrines as action (*karma*), reincarnation (*samsara*), and ethical laws (*dharma*). The word Brahman implies a single, universal spirit, which is why scholars often refer to Brahmanism and Hinduism as monistic religions. Indian monism is also called pantheism (pan = "all"; theist = "god"), which holds that reality consists of only one Being, and that all other forms of reality are appearances of that same Being. Influenced by the doctrine of *samsara*, Buddhists do not speak of the Buddha's life, but rather speak of his many lives. The biography of the Buddha is recounted in *jataka* tales, what Kevin Trainor defines as "accounts of the Buddha's previous lives."[1] In all, there are about 550 *jatakas* outlining the Buddha's previous incarnations, but most non-Buddhists are only aware of his life as Siddharta.[2] As the story goes, Prince Siddhartha's mother, Mahamaya, conceived when a white elephant with six white tusks entered her womb in a dream; Siddhartha later emerged painlessly from her right side and was caught in a golden net by a group of *devas*, or deities. The reader might find the life of the

1. Trainor, *Buddhism*, 22.
2. See Davids, *Stories of the Buddha*.

12

Buddha to appear as legend, or mythological, but one might also consider that the miraculous birth of the New Testament might also sound similarly fantastic to the uninitiated.

Siddhartha Gautama's father, King Shudodhana, realized that his son's birth was extraordinary, and did not want him to grow into a spiritual leader and renounce his inheritance of the kingdom. The king thus protected his son from seeing or experiencing anything that might cause deeper reflections; the realities of suffering and death were shielded from Siddhartha. The *devas* devised an experience, however, that would turn the prince into a spiritual seeker. They arranged that when Siddharta left the palace in his chariot he would for four consecutive days encounter four sights: the first day he saw an old man stooped over his cane (old age); second, he saw a diseased man afflicted with oozing sores (physical suffering); third, he saw a corpse carried in a funeral procession (death); and on the fourth day he saw a wandering ascetic seeking spiritual understanding (spiritual seeking). Despite his father's order that beautiful women seduce him with sensual pleasures, everything Siddhartha perceived spoke "of transience, suffering, and death," and so he renounced society and left the palace at the age of twenty-nine in what Buddhists sometimes call "The Great Departure."[3]

After six years of harsh self-denial, which Siddhartha found ineffective to spiritual insight, he sat beneath a pipal tree, located in modern Bodh Gaya, India, and vowed to remain seated until achieving awakening. According to the *Mahavagga Sutra*, Siddhartha "sat cross-legged for seven days together at the Bo-tree (awakening tree) experiencing the bliss of emancipation," and at the end of the seven days he became enlightened and exclaimed, "Yet for the highest bliss of all, to leave the pride which says 'I am.'"[4] In other words, his final enlightenment occurred once he realized his own non-existence, and it was at that moment under the pipal tree that Siddhartha Gautama became the Buddha, "awakened one." After his awakening he went to the Deer Park at Sarnath, where he gave his first sermon, expounding the principle ideas of Buddhism—the Four Noble Truths and the doctrine of non-existence. It was after this sermon that the Buddhist samgha (community) evolved into being, acquiring a monastic structure and a core of central doctrines.

The Buddha's final act is recorded in the *Parinirvana Sutra*, translated as "discourse on the final extinction." At the end of his life, the Buddha

3. Trainor, *Buddhism*, 29.
4. Warren, *Buddhism in Translations*, 85, 87.

is said to have risen "from the cessation of his perception and sensation, entered the realm of neither perception nor yet non-perception; and rising from the realm of neither perception nor yet non-perception, he entered the realm of nothingness."[5] His final advice to his disciples was that all contingent things pass away, and they should thus strive toward their own awakening with diligence; he offered them no help in the future, for indeed he was transcending into nothingness, which is to be the ultimate aim of his followers. As Kevin Trainor puts it:

> While the Buddha may no longer be directly available to his fol-
> lowers, his liberating presence continues to be manifested in di-
> verse material forms: through his recollected words of instruction;
> contact with pilgrimage sites; and material objects that mediate
> his presence.[6]

The birth, life, teachings, and death of the Buddha could not be more unlike those of Jesus Christ. Jesus proclaimed himself to be the deliverer and way of salvation, whereas the Buddha imparted a set of doctrines helpful toward self-elimination.

Christians cannot fully understand who the Buddha was until an-swering who he was not, and the simple answer to this second question is that he was not Christ, who was God. To better grasp the historical life of the Buddha we need to compare it to the life of Christ. By far the best source of information about the life of Jesus is the New Testament, though some modern scholars today such as Marcus Borg, Bart Erhman, and John Dominic Crossan have challenged the Church's traditional views of Christ's "historical life." Other popular scholars, such as N. T. Wright, Luke Timo-thy Johnson, and Msgr. John P. Meier, argue that the Jesus of faith is empiri-cally shown to be the Jesus of history. But setting aside these acrimonious academic debates, the faith of the Church relies largely on Scripture, as the Word of God, to convey the realities of Jesus' life on earth. Saints Luke and Matthew tell us that Jesus of Nazareth was born in Bethlehem of Judea, and his mother was a virgin.[7] Unlike historical records of the Buddha's life, the childhood years of Jesus remain largely obscure, and the start of his pub-lic ministry began when he was already a grown man, "about thirty years old," at his baptism in the Jordan (Luke 3:23). During his baptism by John the Baptist, "heaven was opened and the Holy Spirit descended on him in

5. Warren, *Buddhism in Translations*, 110.

6. Trainor, *Buddhism*, 41.

7. See Matthew 2, and Luke 2.

bodily form like a dove. And a voice came from heaven: 'You are my Son, whom I love; with you I am well pleased'" (Luke 3:21–22). God, from the skies, so to speak, expressed his favor for his divine Son, who then began to gather followers and preach the Gospel.

Jesus, now grown and gathering his group of twelve apostles, began to fulfill the Messianic prophecies of the Old Testament in word and miracles, outlining the principal beliefs of Christianity and establishing the Christian Church, with Saint Peter as its head. The life of Christ may be divided into Jesus' early ministry when he called his disciples; his preaching and miracles at Galilee; the confession of Saint Peter; the Transfiguration; his final journey into Jerusalem; Holy Week, or his final week in Jerusalem when he was betrayed and arrested; and Jesus' Passion and death. The underlying reality about the life of Christ is that both his identity and message are fundamentally distinct from the Buddha's. To begin with, Jesus, the Son of God, assembled a main group of disciples, not to encourage them to "work out their salvation alone," but rather to provide them with the teachings of the Father and show them the way toward eternal life.

The method in which Jesus called others to himself tells us much of his message. While standing by the Sea of Galilee one day, he asked Simon Peter to borrow his boat, in which he preached to the people gathered on the shore. Then, he said to Simon:

> "Put out into deep water, and let down the nets for a catch." Simon answered, "Master, we've worked hard all night and haven't caught anything. But because you say so, I will let down the nets." When they had done so, they caught such a large number of fish that their nets began to break. So they signaled their partners in the other boat to come and help them, and they came and filled both boats so full that they began to sink. (Luke 5:4–6)

Once he had performed this miracle, Simon Peter, "fell at Jesus' knees and said, 'Go away from me, Lord; I am a sinful man!'" (Luke 5:8). And Jesus responded, "Don't be afraid; from now on you will fish for people" (Luke 5:10). Witnessing this, his first disciples, "pulled their boats up on shore, left everything and followed him" (Luke 5:11). Preaching and miracles attracted followers to Christ, and perhaps even more significant to Jesus' early ministry is Peter's admission of his unworthiness to follow him, for he was "a sinful man." Even at this early stage of his life, Jesus' role as Redeemer from human sin is suggested.

With his disciples at his side, Jesus continued to perform miracles and discourse on his teaching in Galilee. It is during this period that Christ emphasized the importance of faith, one of the hallmarks of the Christian religion, and Peter's attempt to walk on water is one example of the importance of faith in Christianity. After Jesus had joined his disciples in their boat, which "was already a considerable distance from land," and was "buffeted by the waves because the wind was against it," he joined them by walking across the water (Matt 14:22–25). When Peter set out to meet Christ on the water, he only walked part of the way before losing faith and sinking into the lake. "You of little faith," Jesus said, "why did you doubt?" (Matt 14:31). Nowhere in the Buddhist tradition does one find an equivalent of Christ's call for faith.

When Jesus and Peter climbed into the boat, the disciples exclaimed, "Truly you are the Son of God," which is precisely the message of Saint Peter's confession (Matt 14:32). Peter's confession regarding the true nature of Jesus represents perhaps the most critical difference between Jesus and the Buddha. When Jesus and his disciples were in the region of Caesarea Philippi, he asked them, "Who do people say the Son of Man is?" Peter answered, "You are the Messiah, the Son of the living God" (Matt 16: 13–16). Only Peter answers this question correctly, and afterward Christ appointed him head of the community of Christians, the Church. Important here is that Jesus unmistakably announces himself to be the Christ and the Son of God; Jesus, unlike the Buddha, cannot be described as merely "a philosopher," but more rightly as God himself, a member of the Holy Trinity. As if the miracle of walking on water was not enough to unquestionably establish the divinity of Jesus, the Transfiguration, or visual "transformation," demonstrated his human and God nature at once.

Considered to be the "greatest miracle" by Saint Thomas Aquinas, the Transfiguration reconfirmed Jesus' position in the Godhead. As Saint Mark recounts:

> Jesus took Peter, James, and John with him and led them up a high mountain, where they were all alone. There he was transfigured before them. His clothes became dazzling white, whiter than anyone in the world could bleach them. And there appeared before them Elijah and Moses, who were talking with Jesus. (Mark 9: 2–4)

Again, as when Jesus was baptized, "a voice came from the cloud: 'This is my Son, whom I love," and then the voice commanded, "Listen to him!"

(Mark 9:7). Not only is his divinity confirmed, but also is his authority; it is Jesus' voice which we must obey.

After his Transfiguration, Jesus and his disciples entered Jerusalem triumphantly, on a donkey, as "a very large crowd spread their cloaks on the road, while others cut branches from the trees and spread them on the road" as a sign of honor (Matt 21:8). The crowds that went ahead of him and those that followed shouted, "Hosanna to the Son of David!" and "Blessed is he who comes in the name of the Lord!" (Matt 21:9). Towards the end of the week, Jesus shared his "Last Supper" with his disciples and instituted the Eucharist. He was later betrayed in the garden by Judas, arrested, tried by both the Sanhedrin and the Roman prefect of Judea, Pontius Pilate. Then began Jesus' final Passion (suffering), during which he was scourged, crowned with thorns, forced to carry his own cross, and crucified on Golgotha, or the "place of the skull." Jesus' death, according to Christians, marks the center of human history, for it was then that God, Incarnate as Jesus Christ, suffered for the atonement of human sin. Whereas the Buddha was a human teacher, Jesus Christ is teacher, God, and deliverer of all humanity.

In a final word on the comparative identities of the Buddha and Jesus from a Catholic Christian point of view, the Buddha lived many lives until his final extinction, while Jesus lived only once, but exists for all eternity. Christ calls all people to eternity, which only he can provide. Jesus, God made flesh, invites his followers to goodness and peace, and most importantly, to love, and promises to help those who ask him.

Q: How did Buddhism emerge? How did Christianity emerge?

To put it simply, Buddhism consists of the community of believers known as the samgha, which began to grow after Siddhartha became the Buddha. Between the Buddha's awakening (*nirvana*) at the pipal tree and his final extinction (*parinirvana*), his emerging band of followers renounced the world and dispersed to spread his teachings. As new disciples approached the Buddha, he ordained them, calling them bhikkhus, which means "one who lives by alms"; in English bhikkhus are commonly called "monks." Bhikkhus were expected to take a vow to enter the samgha and seek enlightenment. This was the beginning of Buddhist monasticism, though formal monasticism did not begin until later, when bhikkhus began to settle into stable communities. Non-ordained Buddhists were called upasikas, or lay supporters, who were expected to support the samgha and practice what became known as the Five Buddhist Precepts: no killing, no stealing, no sexual misconduct, no lying, and no alcohol. Not long after his great awakening the Buddha had acquired around sixty bhikkhu followers who he commissioned to spread his teachings, making Buddhism one of the most active missionary traditions, along with Christianity and Islam. The Buddha said:

> Travel forth, monks, for the benefit of the many, for the happiness of the many, out of compassion for the world, for the well-being, benefit, and happiness of gods and humans. Two should not go together. Teach, monks, the Dharma which is delightful from beginning to end.[8]

At first, bhikkhus only included men, but after five years the samgha began to include an order of women bhikkhus. The Buddha's aunt and foster mother, Mahaprajapati, asked her nephew if she could be admitted into the samgha, to which he first objected. Legend records that the Buddha's senior disciple, Ananda, intervened on Mahaprajapati's behalf; the Buddha finally agreed to admit her into the community, but only if future nuns consented to eight additional rules that placed the women below the male members of the samgha.

One of the notable aspects of the Buddhist samgha is the principle of the dharmaraja, or "righteous king." This tradition began with the powerful Indian king of the Maurya dynasty (321–185 BC), named Ashoka. In the ninth year of his reign, King Ashoka conquered the small state of Kalinga, massacring more than 100,000 people. This filled him with such remorse as he saw the ravaged bodies of his victims that he converted to Buddhism, and as Kenneth Ch'en writes, "he indulged in no more warfare and devoted the rest of his life to the protection and propagation of the Buddha's teaching."[9] After his conversion, King Ashoka, embarked on a pilgrimage to the sacred sites related to the Buddha and Buddhist history, and he inaugurated the tradition of the "righteous king" who rules as a protector and promoter of the Dharma. In a way, Ashoka was the Constantine of Buddhism, providing the samgha the political support needed to help it spread to new lands.

---

8. Trainor, *Buddhism*, 38.

9. Ch'en, *The Light of Asia*, 112.

The king sent out missionaries who introduced Buddhism to other areas of India and the Far East, Tibet, China, Korea, and eventually Japan.

One of Buddhism's most significant moments was when it entered China during the first century after Christ, where it adopted the cultural and philosophical traditions of China. Relying on Confucianism for its monastic structure and Daoism for its philosophical base, Chinese Buddhism gave the samgha new ways to express the Buddha's teachings, and since China was vastly larger than any other East Asian country, Buddhism expanded into a significant world religion. By the sixth century China's most influential Buddhist school, Chan, was developed, which later traveled into Korea, where it was called Son, and then into Japan, where it was pronounced Zen. Perhaps the most visible form of Buddhism today is Tibetan Buddhism, overseen by the Dalai Lama, which means "ocean of wisdom." The system of Dalai Lamas was not instituted until the fifteenth century, though no Buddhist leader in recent history has been more public than the fourteenth Dalai Lama, who fled Tibet in 1959 during the Tibetan resistance against China's Communist government, which had occupied and incorporated Tibet in 1950.

In essence, then, Buddhism is a religion and philosophy based on the teachings of Siddhartha Gautama, the Buddha, which includes male and female bhikkhus (mendicants/monks/nuns) and non-ordained followers, known as upasikas (lay supporters). While Buddhism does consist of certain central doctrines, it later divided into several schools with varying doctrinal positions. To speak of a Buddhist samgha is no different than to speak of a Christian church; Buddhists, like Christians, are divided regarding what properly constitutes their community of believers, who their leader is, and what their core doctrines are. Zen Buddhism, for example, views all existence as illusory, while Pureland Buddhism accepts that human souls after death can go to places comparable to what Christians imagine as heaven or hell. Whatever one might say about their general similarities, however, the Buddhist samgha, and the Catholic Church are quite different historically and structurally.

Unlike the Buddhist samgha, which formed organically around the historic Buddha, the Catholic Church is considered by Catholics to have been divinely instituted by the One God at Pentecost, during which the Holy Spirit descended upon the Apostles to remain with them as their guide:

> When the day of Pentecost came, they were all together in one
> place. Suddenly a sound like the blowing of a violent wind came
> from heaven and filled the whole house where they were sitting.
> They saw what seemed to be tongues of fire that separated and
> came to rest on each of them. All of them were filled with the Holy
> Spirit and began to speak in other tongues as the Spirit enabled
> them.(Acts 2: 1–4)

In his homily during Pentecost in 1998, Pope Saint John Paul II remarked
that, "With these words the Acts of the Apostles bring us into the heart of
the Pentecost event; they show us the disciples, who, gathered with Mary
in the Upper Room, receive the gift of the Spirit," and thus, "Jesus' promise is fulfilled and the time of the Church begins."[10] In other words, the
Church today is still directed by the same Holy Spirit given to the Apostles
more than two millennia ago, and the successors of those Apostles are the
bishops who still govern the Christian community in their dioceses and
eparchies throughout the world. The most important thing to bear in mind
here is that whereas the Buddhist samgha grew around the Buddha, and
evolved into a more formalized community of monastics and lay followers, Catholics believe the Catholic Church was divinely founded by Jesus
Christ, who is himself God, and the bearer of all truth.

Also unlike the Buddhist samgha, which claims no formal leader—
recall that the institution of the Dalai Lama in Tibetan Buddhism was not
established until the fifteenth century—the Catholic Church was organized
by Christ, the head of the Church, to be led by the successor of Saint Peter,
the bishop of Rome. The Church is, like nature itself, hierarchical, with the
pope established to lead the entire Body of Christians. As the *Catechism of
the Catholic Church* puts it:

> When Christ instituted the Twelve, 'he constituted [them] in the
> form of a college or permanent assembly, at the head of which
> he placed Peter, chosen from among them.' Just as 'by the Lord's
> institution, St. Peter and the rest of the apostles constitute a single
> apostolic college, so in like fashion the Roman Pontiff, Peter's suc-
> cessor, and the bishops, the successors of the apostles, are related
> with and united to one another.'[11]

The two-thousand-year history of apostolic succession, from Christ to today, represents the oldest continuous institution in the history of humanity.

10. John Paul II, Pentecost Homily.
11. *CCC*, 880. Also see Luke 6:13 and John 21:15–17.

Popes, bishops, priests, deacons, religious, and lay, have comprised the Church's structure since its early period, and the papacy has, it is held, under the guidance of the Holy Spirit, safeguarded the deposit of faith given to the first Apostles by Jesus Christ.

Christianity, like Buddhism, has its King Ashoka: the Roman Emperor Constantine. In his famous *Edictum Mediolanense*, or "Edict of Milan" in 313, Constantine decreed that Christians be given legal freedom to practice their faith. The Edict declared:

> Perceiving long ago that religious liberty ought not to be denied, but ought to be granted to the judgment and desire of each individual to perform his religious duties according to his own choice, we had given order that every man, Christians as well as others, should preserve the faith of his own sect and religion. . . . that is, to grant both to the Christians and to all men freedom to follow the religion which they choose, that whatever heavenly divinity exists may be propitious to us and to all that live under our government.[12]

Constantine, as Ashoka was to the Buddhist samgha, also became a great material patron of the Christian church, providing the Christian community the property and financial means to prosper in following centuries.

Another apparent similarity between the Buddhist samgha and the Christian church is the emergence of monasticism, though I should state immediately that the principal goal of Buddhist and Christian monastics is quite different. While Buddhist monks and nuns seek to attain their own awakening, which is essentially an inward activity, Christian monks and nuns direct their entire lives outwardly, toward praising God, the creator and lover of all persons.

The early stages of Christian monasticism began with the Desert Fathers and Mothers who lived mainly in the Scetes desert of Egypt, such as Saint Anthony the Hermit, and reached fulfillment in the West with the Rule of Saint Benedict of Nursia. Circa 530, Saint Benedict, "matured in monastic and spiritual wisdom," put his Rule in order, which Benedict called, "an epitome of Christianity, a learned and mysterious abridgement of all the doctrines of the gospel."[13] Christian monastic life according to the vision of Saint Benedict, was designed to conform to the teachings of Christ

12. Constantine, quoted in Posnov, *History of the Christian Church*, 202.

13. *Compendium of the History of the Cistercian Order*, 8.

as outlined in Scripture, and positioned toward the worship of God and the salvation of souls.

Despite the aesthetic similarities between Catholic and Buddhist monasticism—prayer beads, robes, tonsures, and statues—their orientations are quite different. Buddhist monastics live ascetic lives to gain merit and become detached from the desires and actions (*kharma*) that trap one within the cycle of rebirths; Christian monastics live ascetic lives for penance, prayer, the salvation of souls, and the worship of God. Even the value of silence is viewed differently from a Catholic and Buddhist monastic view; Christian monastics hold that silence helps one better understand the incomprehensible God, whereas Buddhist monks and nuns seek in silence the ultimate emptiness of all. The Buddhist thinker Nagarjuna held that, in the end, silence helps us realize that nothing, ultimately, exists, even ourselves, while the Catholic theologian, Thomas Aquinas, suggested that silence helps clear the veil of noise that obscures God from our senses. As James Fredericks suggests: "Emptiness for Nagarjuna, and incomprehensibility, for Aquinas, are conceptual tools for clarifying what a worthwhile life is for their respective faiths."[14] The difference, again, is that Christian monasticism seeks to know God, whereas Buddhist monasticism seeks largely to apprehend the empty nature of self.

Following Constantine's famous Edict, the growth of monasticism, and the continued advancement of theology during the Middle Ages, the Church became the bedrock and edifice of Western civilization. Its hierarchy, art, architecture, theology, philosophy, scientific study, and social teachings, have remained since Pentecost always, at least ideally, directed toward Jesus Christ, the founder of the Christian community. The nature and goal of the Church is perhaps best described in *Lumen Gentium*, the Dogmatic Constitution of the Church:

> This is the one Church of Christ which in the Creed is professed as one, holy, Catholic and apostolic, which our Savior, after His Resurrection, commissioned Peter to shepherd, and him and the other apostles to extend and direct with authority, which He erected for all ages as "the pillar and mainstay of the truth."[15]

To summarize, whereas the Buddhist samgha could theoretically have emerged and continued without the Buddha, the Christian Church could

---

14. Fredericks, *Buddhists and Christians*, 80.
15. *Lumen Gentium*, 8.

not have been founded or sustained for the last two thousand years were it not for Jesus Christ and his continued involvement.

Q: What are the Four Noble Truths? How do Christians view suffering?

The Four Noble Truths are at the very center of the Buddha's teachings, and indeed they were the topic of his first sermon after achieving enlightenment. In essence, each of the Four Noble Truths, perhaps the entire Buddhist tradition, focuses on the elimination of human suffering, which is called *dukkha*. It is remarkable how different are the Buddhist and Catholic understandings of suffering; for Buddhists suffering is universally bad, while Catholic Christians recognize its intrinsic value when connected to the virtues of self-sacrifice and self-denial. We can summarize the Four Noble Truths in the following: First, all is suffering (*dukkha*); second, the cause of suffering is craving; third, the cessation of suffering, which is achieved by the elimination of all craving; and fourth, craving can be eliminated by following the Eightfold Path. The Eightfold Path consists of eight practices that facilitate the eradication of craving, such as right speech, right action, and so forth.[16] Perhaps the best source for this teaching is the famous *Turning the Wheel of Dharma Sutra*.

In this sutra, the Buddha describes in detail what he means by suffering and how to relinquish it:

> Now, monks, what is the Noble Truth of suffering: Just this: Birth is suffering, old age is suffering, sickness is suffering, death is suffering. Involvement with what is unpleasant is suffering. Separation from what is pleasant is suffering. Also, not getting what one wants and strives for is suffering. And form (*rupa*) is suffering, feeling (*vedana*) is suffering, perception (*samjna*) is suffering, karmic constituents (*samskaras*) are suffering, consciousness (*vijnana*) is suffering.[17]

What he is saying is that anything that elicits any form of response, positive or negative, is in the end a form of suffering, for even pleasure causes one to either desire more pleasure (which causes suffering) or fear that the pleasure will end (which is un-pleasurable). The Buddhist view that *everything*

16. For a good description of the Four Noble Truths and the components of the Eightfold Path, see Robinson, *Buddhist Religions*, 27–31.

17. Translated in Strong, *The Experience of Buddhism*, 43.

conditioned by *karma* is suffering is to be taken literally, which is a very foreign notion to most Westerners, and especially Catholics.

When discussing the Second Noble Truth, the Buddha describes craving as, "the thirst for further existence, which comes along with pleasure and passion and brings passing enjoyment here and there."[18] Attachment to self, attachment to one's existential being, is according to the Buddha, the bedrock of suffering, and the only way to escape suffering is to eliminate craving, which is facilitated by the very act of being. He says that the cessation of suffering consists of, "the destruction without remainder of this very thirst for further existence, which comes along with pleasure and passion."[19] Buddhist enlightenment, or *nirvana*, is precisely this, the complete extinction of self, which I will discuss more below. And finally, the Fourth Noble Truth is the way leading to the elimination of craving and the final cessation of suffering, the Eightfold Path.

Even more complicated than the Four Noble Truths is the application of the Eightfold Path: right views, right intention, right speech, right action, right livelihood, right effort, right mindfulness, and right concentration. The Buddhist scholar, Edward Conze, has offered one of the simplest summaries of what this doctrine recommends. He notes that right views merely imply the mental adoption of the Four Noble Truths, and the path of right intentions suggests "a desire for self-extinction and the welfare of others," and right effort "refers to one's endeavors to abandon unwholesome dharmas."[20] By "unwholesome dharmas" Conze means any teaching that causes craving and suffering, or more precisely, any teaching other than Buddhism. The reader may have noticed that the Four Noble Truths point toward a suspicion and dislike of human existence as the ultimate cause of unhappiness, and this is correct. In a Buddhist commentary known as the *Visuddhimagga*, or "path of purification," it is proposed that craving depends on existence, and one of the arguments made in this text is that all action (*karma*) causes one to persist in being and craving.[21] To finally escape suffering one must finally escape being, which runs against some of the foundations of Catholic belief.

18. Strong, *The Experience of Buddhism*, 44.

19. Ibid.

20. Conze, *Buddhism*, 48.

21. For an excerpt from the Visuddhimagga, see Warren, *Buddhism in Translations*, 194–201.

As in all other comparisons between Christianity and Buddhism, the nature of anything, such as suffering and joy, is affected by whether or not one believes in a monotheistic God, or creator. James Fredericks put it succinctly: "Buddhism, unlike Christianity, has no notion of the 'Maker of heaven and earth,' the Creator-God who has brought the world into being and who one day will bring creation to an end." "Instead," Fredericks notes, "Buddhism imagines reality to be the cause of itself, with no God beyond it as its transcendent Creator."[22] Simply said, for Buddhists there is no God to make sense of or transform suffering; humans are left alone to confront their own anguish. In general, there are three fundamental Catholic answers to the Buddhist understanding of being human and the condition of suffering, all of which rest on the belief that we are not alone, and that God is present to mitigate all human sorrow and afflictions. First, humanity was made in God's image, and thus a human being is something to be celebrated rather than lamented; second, suffering helps us better understand Christ, who transforms suffering into joy; and third, craving, in itself can be holy, and can lead to greater holiness and wisdom.

The dignity of humanity is asserted in the Creation account in Genesis, for man was made in the divine likeness and image of God himself: "When God created mankind, he made them in the likeness of God. He created them male and female and blessed them. And he named them 'Mankind' when they were created" (Gen 5:1–3). In commenting on the Creation narrative, Father James Scullion, OFM, writes that, "To be created in the 'likeness and image of God' (Gen 1:26–27) means to be a little lower than God, crowned with glory and honor."[23] While one might argue that this does not entirely mitigate human suffering, the Catholic belief holds that our dignity, having been made in the image of God, provides humanity with a powerful incentive to bear suffering with the knowledge that we were created for something better, something that God has promised to fulfill if we "stay the course." To be precise, God did not make humanity in his image to be, as Buddhism attempts to do, erased. Indirectly addressing this point, Peter Kreeft, in his book, *Making Sense Out of Suffering*, says:

> I am not a Buddhist. I cannot help viewing *Nirvana* [erasure] as spiritual euthanasia, killing the patient (the self, the I, the ego) to cure the disease (egotism, selfishness). Buddhism eliminates the I that hates and suffers, yes; but that is also the I that loves. . . .

22. Fredericks, *Buddhists and Christians*, 43–44.
23. Scullion, "Creation-Incarnation," 11.

> Buddha seems to be simply unaware of the possibility of unselfish love, unselfish will, unselfish passion, and unselfish self.[24]

I add to Kreeft's insightful statement, that "the I" that the Buddha seems most unaware of is "the I" that was created in God's image, that is capable of unselfish love, love that endures and transforms all suffering, precisely because humanity was made in God's likeness.

Christianity also disagrees with the Buddhist notion that all suffering is bad, and to be escaped from. John Paul II has noted in his trenchant work on the nature of evil and suffering, *Salvifici Doloris*, that it is largely through suffering that human beings are joined to the pain of Christ. As Cardinal Javier Lozano Barragán summarized the pope's assertion in his lecture, "A Christian Understanding of Pain and Suffering":

> Through suffering, human beings are incorporated into the pain of Christ. Suffering gives rise to love for those who suffer, a disinterested love to help them by relieving it. This is now official and organized through health-care institutions and the professionals who work in them, and also through volunteers. It is a matter of a real vocation, especially when one is united to the Church with a Christian profession.[25]

In other words, among its many functions, suffering can be transformed into something good; by being "incorporated into the pain of Christ," we learn to better love those who suffer. An excellent example of the compassion (co-suffering) is seen in the Christian parable of the Samaritan. While the priest and the Levite pass by the half-dead man along their way, leaving him to die alone, the Samaritan, on the other hand, "saw him and had compassion on him. He went to him, . . . and bound up his wounds," and then "brought him to an inn, and took care of him" (Luke 10: 33–34). Compassion in the Christian sense is inspired not because of its view that suffering is in all cases bad, as in Buddhist teaching, but because suffering can be a means of sympathy and oneness with Christ, who transforms all things into good. John Paul II has argued that, "The mystery of the Redemption of the world is in an amazing way rooted in suffering, and this suffering in turn finds in the mystery of the Redemption its supreme and surest point of reference."[26]

24. Kreeft, *Making Sense Out of Suffering*, 4.
25. Barragán, "A Christian Understanding of Pain and Suffering."
26. John Paul II, *Salvifici Doloris*, 31.

And finally, in contrast to the Buddhist notion that all craving causes suffering, the Christian responds that holy and good longing causes holy and good results. Christians might agree with Buddhists that desire is often better than satisfaction—that we are often disappointed when we get what we hoped for—there are some desires, such as the desire for God, that exceed expectations when they are attained. Also, as Father Ronald Rolheiser notes, "Desire makes us act," and if our desires are for good things, then our actions are good.[27] While we often associate desire with erotic or sexual cravings, there are other directions to which desire can lead. Imagine Mother Teresa. She spoke of desire as "hunger," and shows how this hunger can be transformative in a world full of suffering:

> There is a terrible hunger for love. We all experience that in our lives—the pain, the loneliness. We must have the courage to recognize it. The poor you may have right in your own family.[28]

Our "hunger" for love, she suggests, makes us more compassionate, and more holy if our hunger turns into holy action.

In a final word about suffering, the Christian does not share the Buddhist belief that nothing is permanent, and that suffering is largely a result of this impermanence. For the Buddhist, "the world is nothing more than one utterly momentary state of affairs passing into another," and thus attachment, even to what is good, causes suffering once what is enjoyed passes away.[29] God as viewed in Christianity, however, never changes, and what he promises will never change. The Buddhist view that all things are illusory is, paradoxically, an illusion. In Christianity there is permanence, and it is in this divine Permanence that all suffering passes. Saint Augustine, who understood the inconsistent and tormented nature of the human mind, has said perhaps better than anyone what is the true answer to human suffering:

> Great are you, O Lord, and exceedingly worthy of praise; your power is immense, and your wisdom beyond reckoning. And so we men, who are a due part of your creation, long to praise you— we also carry our mortality about with us, carry the evidence of our sin and with it the proof that you thwart the proud. You arouse us so that praising you may bring us joy, because you have made

---

27. Rolheiser, *Holy Longing*, 7.

28. Quoted in Partner, *Quicknotes*, 105.

29. Fredericks, *Buddhists and Christians*, 44.

us and drawn us to yourself, and our heart is unquiet until it rests in you.[30]

Q: What makes a person a Buddhist? What makes a person a Christian?

Despite the proliferation of Buddhist statues, Zen candles, desk-sized Zen gardens, and Buddhist "prayer" mats in American superstores, creating a peaceful, Zen-scented atmosphere in one's apartment or home does not make one a Buddhist. Even more common than Buddhist décor is the Western assumption that one can claim to be Buddhist, the "safe religion," without formal affiliation to, or training in, the samgha. This form of "armchair," or "strip mall," Buddhism for spiritual "seekers" who dislike "organized religion" and "denominational" membership may be, as one can imagine, disconcerting to actual Buddhists. It is like, but not exactly like, a person claiming to be Catholic while rejecting the papacy, sacraments, and Church hierarchy, simply because he or she finds rosaries, crucifixes, and Marian statues aesthetically attractive. Buddhism, like Catholicism, requires formal steps of initiation and entrance into the official structure of the community. How odd Tibetan "prayer flags" appear to actual Tibetan Buddhists, who know them to be *sutra* banners, traditionally placed in areas known to be inhabited by a powerful *deva*, or spirit, rather than front porches or college dorm rooms. Similarly, Catholic Christians are often surprised to see rosaries worn as a fashion accessory.

When asked what makes a person Buddhist the Dalai Lama insists that one can be considered Buddhist only after taking the vow of the Three Refuges.[31] While Buddhism has nothing comparable to Christian sacraments, it does have a long tradition of ritual and doctrinal formulas, and one of the principle rites of entrance into the Buddhist community is the vow to follow the Three Refuges, or the Triple Gem (or Jewel) Oath: "I take refuge in the Buddha; I take refuge in the Dharma; I take refuge in the Samgha." What is implied in this vow is complete compliance with the historic Buddha, his teaching, and the community of followers who have also taken this oath, but it also means that the new Buddhist has promised to

---

30. Excerpted from the *Confessions of St. Augustine*, book I, chapter 1.

31. See, for example, *The Dalai Lama, Tenzin Gyatso, The Dalai Lama at Harvard*, trans. by Jeffrey Hopkins (Ithaca: Snow Lion, 1988), 15.

take sanctuary in Buddhism rather than other faith traditions. Buddhism is not, as some suppose, religiously inclusive. Edward Conze notes that this formula has been recited for over 2,500 years, and is accompanied by the commitment to follow the Five Precepts.

Catholicism and Buddhism do in fact intersect in the tenets of the Five Precepts, which some consider to be a shortened version of the Christian Ten Commandments. After taking refuge in the Buddha (awakened one), Dharma (teaching), and Samgha (community), the newly initiated Buddhist promises to, as John Strong puts it, "abstain from killing, stealing, unchastity, lying, and drinking intoxicants."[32] And in some cases, laypersons also pledge "not to eat after noon, to abstain from going to public entertainments and from adorning their persons in any way, and not to use high or broad beds (that is, to sit on mats on the floor)."[33] Buddhists who later become monks or nuns are required to take additional vows, including the promise to abstain from having or using money. It is important to bear in mind that authentic Buddhism requires its followers to choose between being Buddhist or a follower of another religion, such as Christianity, and this is accomplished by requiring Buddhists to adopt the Three Refuges and follow the Five Precepts.

In addition, a Buddhist is expected to apply himself to what the fifth-century Buddhist writer, Buddhaghosa, called the two "legs" of Buddhism, morality and meditation, "upon which the 'body' of liberating insight stands."[34] Not only are Buddhist followers expected to obey the Five Precepts, but they are also hoped to practice regular meditation techniques intended to facilitate the proper mental state to attain *nirvana*. Perhaps the best explanation of Buddhist meditation is found in the work of the second-century BC Indian teacher, Patanjali, who wrote that, "Meditation is stilling the fluctuations of consciousness."[35] For Catholic Christians, one sees similarities between Buddhist and Catholic morality, but to be a Buddhist is to depart from Catholic teaching in the areas of Three Refuges and the practice of mental states to facilitate self-extinction, for the very goals of Buddhist meditation are to erase the mental distinctions of self and other.

Certainly, just as there are many forms and schools of Buddhism, each one differing slightly in how it would define "being a Buddhist," Christianity

32. Strong, *The Experience of Buddhism*, 120.

33. Ibid.

34. Todd T. Lewis, "The Path of the Buddha," in Trainor, 72.

35. Patanjali, Yogasutras, 1.2. Quoted in Wallis, *The Dhammapada*, 115, note 27.

also, with its proliferation of denominations, varies in its opinions of what it means to "be a Christian." From the Catholic point of view, a Christian is one who believes that Jesus Christ is the Son of God and follows his teachings, and in a more complete sense, a Christian professes the faith as expressed in the Apostles Creed. The Church's Dogmatic Constitution, *Dei Verbum*, has pointed to the necessity of believing in the divine nature of Scripture, which is the revelation of God's Word to mankind, and has thus said that: "By this revelation then, the deepest truth about God and the salvation of man shines forth in Christ, who is at the same time the mediator and the fullness of all revelation."[36] And furthermore, to be Christian is to see in Jesus Christ the "Word made flesh, sent 'as a man to men,'" who, "speaks the words of God" (John 3:34). As this is expressed in *Dominus Iesus* as, "To see Jesus is to see the Father."[37]

Catholics also believe that to be Christian in the whole sense is to be a member of the Catholic Church, inside of which one may benefit from the fullness of the sacraments given to created persons by God through his priests. In contrast to the Buddhist vow of commitment to the Three Refuges, Christians enter into the Christian community through the sacrament of baptism, which is administered in the name of the Holy Trinity: the Father, Son, and Holy Spirit. Based largely on Saint John's statement that, "Truly, truly, I say to you, unless one is born of water and the Spirit, he cannot enter into the Kingdom of God" (John 3:34), the Church views baptism as, with some theological nuances, essential for both the entrance into Christianity and for the spiritual salvation of one's soul. To clarify this, the *Catechism of the Catholic Church* states that, "Baptism is necessary for salvation for those to whom the Gospel has been proclaimed and who have had the possibility of asking for this sacrament."[38]

Once baptized, the Catholic Christian enters into the sacramental life of the Church as a member of the Body of Christ; Christians understand themselves to be members of the same spiritual Body, about which Saint Robert Bellarmine said, "we form one Church and one Body, united by the bond of the same charity in the Kingdom of Christ."[39] To be a Christian, then, is to be a mystical part of the One Body of Christ, into which one is joined through baptism, and within which one enjoys the graces imparted

36. *Dei Verbum*, 2.
37. *Dominus Iesus*, 5.
38. *CCC*, 261.
39. St. Robert Bellarmine, SJ, *De Indulgentiis*, lib. I, cap. 14.

through the sacraments. Buddhists define themselves by membership within the Buddhist samgha, and Christians identify themselves by their membership in the Christian Church; to claim a dual membership in both communities is to misunderstand and, perhaps, distort the teachings of both Christianity and Buddhism. To be authentically Christian is believe in Christ as the perfect mediator of truth and salvation, and to receive his grace in the wholeness of the faith found in the Catholic Church. One cannot, according to these tenets, be both Christian and Buddhist. In *Redemptoris Missio*, Pope John Paul II made this point quite cogently when he said that various strands of mediation that are apparent in other religious faith traditions, such as Buddhism, "acquire meaning and value *only* from Christ's own mediation, and they cannot be understood as parallel or complimentary to his."[40] The Christian understanding of the Holy Spirit is not unknown to many Buddhists, and Christians hold that this Spirit is always calling non-Christians into the truth, toward the visible community of Christians, which is the Church. Saint John Chrysostom astutely reminded the Christians of his era that the Church will always remain visible and open to non-believers: "It is an easier thing for the sun to be quenched than for the Church to be made invisible."[41]

Q: Why do some Catholics and Buddhists today show interest in mixing these two religions?

Buddhism was already fashionable in America by the mid-1950s, and when Jack Kerouac's 1958 novel, *The Dharma Bums*, launched the beat generation toward global popularity, the appeal of Eastern religion drew Western teenagers into an alternative form of spirituality. In this autobiographical novel, Kerouac, under the pseudonym Ray Smith, describes his spiritual awakening:

> I believed that I was an oldtime bhikku [Buddhist monk] in modern clothes wandering the world (usually the immense triangular arc of New York to Mexico City to San Francisco) in order to turn the wheel of True Meaning, or Dharma, and gain merit for myself as a future Buddha (Awak-ener) and as a future Hero in Paradise.[42]

40. John Paul II, *Redemptoris Missio*, 5.
41. Quoted in Hunter, *Outlines of Dogmatic Theology*, 169.
42. Kerouac, *The Dharma Bums*, 5.

A renowned progenitor of the beatniks, Kerouac, is one of a long list of celebrity authors who either converted to Buddhism from Christianity, or simply combined the two. The well-known and ingenious British writer and child of missionary parents, Alan Watts, famously converted to Buddhism, was later ordained an Anglican priest, and left the ministry to pursue a more eclectic spiritual path, more Zen than Christian.[43]

Nearly a half century before Kerouac and Watts began their spiritual journeys, America hosted an event that made Buddhism a household word, the World's Parliament of Religions, convened at the 1893 Chicago Exposition. The Japanese abbot, Soyen Shaku, was invited to attend the Parliament, and he became the first Zen priest to publically visit the United States; his speech was translated into English by his disciple, the brilliant Buddhist scholar, D. T. Suzuki. Open Court publisher, Paul Carus, was so impressed by Soyen's speech that he asked him to send an English-speaking Buddhist master to introduce Buddhism to America. Soyen sent D. T. Suzuki, who hit America like a thunderstorm, publishing scores of books and translations on Zen and other Buddhist schools. Most Americans were exposed to the sutras for the first time, and Suzuki himself attracted some of the West's most creative thinkers, such twentieth-century luminaries as John Cage, Erich Fromm, Karen Horney, Aldous Huxley, and Carl Jung. But by far the most influential admirer was the Trappist monk and Roman Catholic priest, Thomas Merton.

After reading Suzuki's works, Merton began to view Zen as a necessary supplement to Christianity, which he felt had forfeited its mysticism in favor of modern materialism. So taken by Suzuki's Buddhism was Merton, that in his own book, *Zen and the Birds of Appetite*, he exclaimed that, "Christian renewal has meant that Christians are now wide open to Asian religions," though his optimism was not entirely blind to difference.[44] When asking if it is "possible to say that both Christians and Buddhists can equally well practice Zen," he responds, "Yes," while admitting that, "On the theological level the question becomes more complex."[45] D. T. Suzuki was also well aware of these differences, writing in a letter to Merton that the Zen-man has "no God that corresponds to the analogical Christian

---

43. For a discussion of figures such as Alan Wats and other popular modern Buddhists see Eric Cunningham, *Zen Past and Present*, especially chapter 8.

44. Merton, *Zen and the Birds of Appetite*, 15.

45. Ibid., 44.

God."[46] In Suzuki's Buddhist view, opposites are human inventions; there is no good and evil, right and wrong, life and death, truth and falsehood, and no creator or created.[47]

Despite these distinctions, Merton's growing attraction to Buddhism seems to have blurred, rather than clarified, the line between Christianity and Buddhism. In his *Asian Journal*, Father Merton recorded a dream:

> I was dressed in a Buddhist monk's habit, but with more black and red and gold, a "Zen habit," in color more Tibetan than Zen. . . .
> I met some women in the corridor, visitors and students of Asian religion, to whom I was explaining I was a kind of Zen monk and Gelugpa together, when I woke up.[48]

This may be the first record of a Catholic monk dreaming of being a Buddhist monk. Merton's explorations into Buddhist writings in his Trappist hermitage later became an exploration into Buddhist temples in Asian countries, and his quick friendship with the Dalai Lama not only heralded a new era of productive Christian-Buddhist dialogue and friendship, but perhaps also a new era of Christian-Buddhist syncretism.

While Jack Kerouac helped make Buddhism an alternative spiritual path to Catholicism, Thomas Merton, perhaps quite unintentionally, helped make Buddhism a complimentary spiritual path to present and future Catholics. Today, members of both the Buddhist samgha and Catholic Church have formed organizations that follow in the footsteps of Father Thomas Merton. The Los Angeles Buddhist Samgha Council and the Catholic Office of Ecumenical and Interreligious Dialogue host events to connect Catholics and Buddhists for interfaith dialogue, and Benedictine and Trappist monks and nuns have established the organization, Monastic Interreligious Dialogue, to facilitate Catholic-Buddhist events. Several of these gatherings included the Dalai Lama's teachings on such Buddhist scriptures as the *Heart Sutra*, which imparts the Buddhist doctrine of impermanence, or non-existence. Not only has Buddhism become a popular venue for dialogue—or common "worship"—Buddhist teaching has become a common platform for spiritual reading and practice at Catholic retreat centers.

46. Ibid., 103.
47. Ibid., 103.
48. Merton, *Asian Journals*, 107.

The Jesuit priest, Father Robert Kennedy, SJ, is one of the more prominent inheritors of Thomas Merton's legacy. Kennedy is both an ordained Roman Catholic priest and Zen priest, former chair of the Theology Department of St. Peter's University, Jersey City, New Jersey, and author of *Zen Gifts to Christians* and *Zen Spirit, Christian Spirit*. Kennedy leads Zen practitioners in morning meditation at his Morning Star Zendo. He also transmits Buddhist teachings to disciples, and has ordained other Roman Catholic priests into his lineage, including Father Patrick Eastman, founder of the Wild Goose Samgha, and Father Kevin Hunt, a Trappist monk. Do such popular books as Father William Johnston's, SJ, *Christian Zen*, or Kim Boykin's *Zen for Christians*, represent what the Second Vatican Council really had in mind when the Council Fathers discussed the Church's relationship with other religions? This remains a hotly-debated question among Catholic intellectuals, both in the so-called progressive and conservative camps.

While there are some Catholics and Buddhists who advocate a mixture of Christianity and Buddhism as a new hybrid religion, we must bear in mind that the Church's official position regarding Buddhism is in fact distant from such a vision. It would be more accurate to describe the Church's view of Buddhism as morally commendable in areas, but essentially incompatible with the fundamental teachings Christ bestowed to the Church. When then Cardinal Joseph Ratzinger was invited to St. Patrick's Seminary in Menlo Park, California, to deliver a talk to American Catholic educators in 1999, Ratzinger is reported to have remarked that Buddhism is an "autoerotic spirituality" that seeks "transcendence without imposing concrete religious obligations."[49] He also reportedly noted that, "Buddhism would replace Marxism as the church's biggest foe by 2000," a point that has been made by several other prominent Catholic thinkers.[50] While some Western reporters have criticized the cardinal's use of the term, "autoerotic," to describe Buddhism, they have failed to note that his original use of the expression appeared in a French publication, wherein the term appears as "auto-erotisme," which means "self-absorption" or "self-focused." This is very different from what is implied in the English usage, and reflects the Church's understanding of Buddhist doctrine and its distinction from Christian belief, which is essentially outwardly focused.

49. Heng Sure, "Pope Benedict XVI's Buddhist Encounter."
50. Ibid.

It will serve to clarify what the Church actually says about Buddhism in order to dispel the common misconception that it is possible, or even preferable, to mix Buddhism with Catholic Christianity. I have already quoted from the Church's authoritative statement on other religions, Vatican II's *Nostra Aetate*; it is from this document that the Church speaks most clearly about Christianity's place vis-à-vis Buddhism. *Nostra Aetate* states that:

> Buddhism, in its various forms, realizes the radical insufficiency of this changeable world; it teaches a way by which men, in a devout and confident spirit, may be able either to acquire the state of perfect liberation, or attain, by their own efforts or through higher help, supreme illumination.

It continues to suggest that, "The Catholic Church rejects nothing that is true and holy in these religions," and believes that other religions can at times "reflect a ray of that Truth which enlightens all men." While many who quote this text to support their ambition to combine these two religions stop at this point in the passage, the document continues in saying that the Church "proclaims, and ever must proclaim Christ 'the way, the truth, and the life' (John 14:6), in whom men may find the fullness of religious life, in whom God has reconciled all things to Himself."[51] Certainly, and unequivocally, the Council affirmed that Buddhism may contain a ray of "Truth," though it does not approve the misappropriation of Buddhist beliefs into Christian practice. What the Council does assert is that non-Catholic religions can be fulfilled only through the truths held exclusively by the Church.

One of the common charges of Christians who argue in favor of introducing Buddhism into the theology and practice of Christianity is that the Church does not understand what Buddhism "really teaches." This is necessarily untrue. The Church's International Theological Commission, in 1995, confronted the question of the Catholic belief in Christ as Savior in contrast to other world religions, which resulted in the wonderfully lucid exposition of Buddhism compared to the Catholic "theology of the Redeemer."

The first comment the Commission makes about Buddhism concerns the Buddha's view of scripture and metaphysics—the nature of God—in contrast to Catholic doctrine. The Commission stated:

51. See *Nostra Aetate*, 2.

As regards Buddhism, one can begin by saying that Buddha, in dealing with the suffering of the world, rejected the authority of the *Vedas*, the usefulness of sacrifices, and saw no use either in metaphysical speculations about the existence of God and the soul. He sought deliverance from suffering from within man himself. His central insight is that human desire is the root of all evil and misery—which in turn gives rise to "ignorance" (*avidya*)—and the ultimate cause of the cycle of birth and rebirth.[52]

In other words, this official document stated in 1995 what Cardinal Ratzinger was merely reiterating in 1999, namely, that Buddhism is principally an inwardly focused religion, in which deliverance is sought "from within man himself."

After an edifying discussion of the Buddhist ideas regarding non-permanence (*anicca*) and appearance (*maya*), the Commission addresses the Buddhist version of "salvation," or *nirvana*. Buddhist "redemption," the document describes, consists of the following: "Being radically other than the transitory torment of this world of *Maya*, Nirvana—literally: 'extinction' or 'going out' (i.e., of all desires), as the light of a candle goes out when the wax has been burned away."[53] Admitting that *nirvana* "is not an intellectual goal but an experience that is indefinable," the Commission notes that what can be clearly discerned from Buddhist teaching is that it "places all its emphasis on human efforts"; a conceptual realization of God, and his divine teachings, are conspicuously absent from Buddhist teaching.[54] In a final note on Buddhism, the document acknowledges that, "From the perspective of Buddhism all other religious paths are imperfect and secondary," which, in all fairness, is precisely the Catholic Christian view of religions other than itself.[55]

The Church continues to recognize God's light when and where it appears in all spiritual inquiry, whether in Buddhism or any other religious tradition that seeks truth, but even more importantly, it reaffirms that Christ, who is the Truth, has not left his Church lacking and in need of supplementation. John Paul II, in his Apostolic Letter, *Tertio Millenio Adveniente*, discussed the Church in Asian countries, where there "is a great challenge for evangelization, since religious systems such as Buddhism or

52. International Theological Commission, "Select Questions on the Theology of the Redeemer," Part I, 20.

53. Ibid., Part I, 22.

54. Ibid., Part I, 22.

55. Ibid.

Hinduism have a clearly soteriological [salvific] character." What is therefore vital, the Pope urged, is to in these countries "illustrate and explain
more fully the truth that Christ is the one Mediator between God and man
and the sole Redeemer of the world, to be clearly distinguished from the
founders of other great religions."[56] To summarize Catholic teaching on
Buddhism and other non-Christian religions, we can assert that to look
outwardly to another religious tradition is to mistakenly assume, directly
or indirectly, that the religious belief and practice bestowed to the Church
by Jesus Christ, is somehow deficient.

Before one turns to the "Buddhist-Christianities" popularized by people such as Jack Kerouac, Allan Watts, and others, I recommend a careful
and broad understanding of what Christ and the Church have taught. Most
who have turned to "alternative spiritualities" to supplement their Christian
faith are likely to discover what they seek is already within the long and rich
tradition of the Church. Chesterton's quip that, "The Christian ideal has not
been tried and found wanting. It has been found difficult and left untried,"
applies just as much to those within the Church as to those without.[57]

Q: What is "Zen Catholicism"?

Despite the growing number of online blogs and web addresses that use
the term "Zen Catholicism" to describe a form of Buddhist Catholicism (or
Catholic Buddhism), there is no such thing. Zen and Catholicism are two
distinct religions. The term is derived from a book by that title published
in 1963 by the Benedictine priest at Britain's Ampleforth Abbey, Father
Aelred Graham, OSB, who corresponded often with Thomas Merton. Graham's book, *Zen Catholicism*, was written after he had retired and made a
trip to the Far East, where he met Buddhist and Hindu leaders. One of the
principle themes of *Zen Catholicism* is that the deepest teachings of Zen
Buddhism are the same as the deepest roots of Catholicism, and in fact,
Graham suggests that the light of Zen is necessary to illuminate the hidden
areas of Catholicism. Knowing that some Catholics might be suspicious of
his attempt at religious syncretism, Graham states that, "in applying certain
insights from Zen to Catholicism, we shall be in no danger of confusion."[58]
This is so because, as he assures his reader, "Zen is not a theology; it has

56. John Paul II, *Tertio Millenio Adveniente*, 38.

57. Chesterton, *What's Wrong with the World?*, 48.

58. Graham, *Zen Catholicism*, 20.

nothing to tell us about a supernatural revelation, nothing therefore that needs to be 'corrected.'"[59]

Merton, Graham, Kennedy, and several other Catholic priests who appear to advocate the use of Zen as an alternative, or supplemental, form of "prayer" often insist in their works that Zen is not a threat to Catholic belief because it is "not a theology" or "religion." While this assertion is not entirely incorrect, it is misleading, and it will be useful to outline a few of the basic ideas expressed in Zen Buddhism to demonstrate how distant Zen's teachings are from those of the Catholic Church. First, while Zen is often imagined as a Japanese form of Buddhism, it was first established in China, where it was called Chan, the Chinese transliteration of the Indian term *dyana*, or "meditation."[60] There is no mystery behind the appeal of Zen Buddhism among Catholics interested in deepening their prayer life, for Zen's specialty is sitting contemplation. The putative founder of Zen was the Indian monk, Bodhidharma, who in the sixth century, as Buddhist scholar Peter Harvey notes, "spent nine years in meditation gazing at a wall, until his legs fell off!"[61] Another legend records that he once fell asleep while meditating and was so agitated that he cut off his own eyelids to avoid dosing off again—his eyelids grew into tea leaves, which were infused by the other monks to remain alert during meditation. All such Zen legends reinforce the underlining value of sitting meditation, which employs deep contemplation to attain awakening.

The fundamental goal of *zazen*, or Zen sitting, is to become aware of the reality that there is, paradoxically, no reality to become aware of. Paradox is the foundation of Zen sitting, which can be expressed in the story of how Huineng became China's Chan patriarch in the eighth century. When the fifth patriarch, Hongren, set out to find a successor he invited his disciples to compose *gathas*, or short Buddhist hymns, as a form of competition. Huineng wrote this:

> Bodhi originally has no tree;
> the mirror has no stand.
> Buddha nature is always clean and pure;
> where is there room for dust?[62]

59. Ibid., 18.
60. See Gregory, *Traditions of Meditation*, 207.
61. Harvey, *An Introduction to Buddhism*, 153.
62. Translated Yampolsky, *Platform Sutra of the Sixth Patriarch*, 132.

In Buddhist terms, a lot is implied in Huineng's insightful *gatha*: First, he denies the Bodhi, or "enlightenment" tree that the Buddha meditated under; second, he denies the classical image of the "mirror," with which one sees oneself; third, he denies the purity of the Buddha nature, or the state of enlightenment; and fourth, he denies the "dust" that obscures enlightenment. In essence, Huineng's brief verse conveys the Zen idea that meditation brings one to an understanding that Buddhism itself is unreal.

Zen is an extremely complicated tradition, so complicated in fact that Merton, Kennedy, and others appear to have overlooked the reason that Zen is not a theology, which is because it denies the possibility, or relevance, of a God (*theos*); it is not concerned with supernatural revelation because it dismisses the supernatural and revelation as illusions; and it cannot be corrected because, as Huineng asserts, there is ultimately nothing within the realm of existence to correct. Graham's argument that Zen is benign to Christianity because it is not a theology is incorrect; Zen's rejection of theology is precisely what renders it problematic. Whether or not Graham and Merton believed Zen to be a bona fide religion, it functions as one when practiced. The goal of Zen teaching is so elusive as to deny logical thought from any conclusions—final answers are impossible. As Harvey puts it, in Zen "the ultimate level of truth is expressed: all phenomenon, however exalted, are empty."[63] One of Zen's trademarks is its reliance on Chinese Daoism, a philosophy that rejects the possibility of all truth claims, for according to this view language and all linguistic distinctions are delusions.

A favorite philosopher among Zen practitioners is the Daoist writer Zhuangzi, who lived during China's fourth century BC. Zhuangzi's most famous anecdote is his clever butterfly dream:

> Once upon a time Zhuangzi dreamed that he was a butterfly, a butterfly flitting about happily enjoying himself. He didn't know that he was Zhuangzi. Suddenly he awoke and was palpably Zhuangzi. He did not know whether he was Zhuangzi who had dreamed of being a butterfly or a butterfly dreaming that he was Zhuangzi.[64]

This story is attractive to Zen Buddhism precisely because it rejects the possibility of distinguishing real from false, which begs the question; if Zen practice teaches one that truth is unknowable and reality is an illusion, can it appropriately function as a helpful intellectual compliment to Catholic

---

63. Harvey, *Introduction to Buddhism*, 155.

64. Translated in Mair, *Wandering on the Way*, 24. I have re-transliterated Chuang Chou to his more commonly known name, Zhuangzi, for the sake of clarity.

spiritual practice and belief? The great sixteenth-century Catholic missionary to China, Matteo Ricci, SJ, who perhaps understood Buddhist teaching better than many modern scholars, made a career of disputing Buddhist doctrines, though he sometimes did so with less charity than hoped for. In his most famous book, *The True Meaning of the Lord of Heaven*, Ricci asserts that, "The mistakes made by Buddhists are beyond reckoning," and he continues to state that the Buddha and the Daoist founder, Laozi, "have made a great number of false statements in their comments on the most important of matters."[65] Centuries later, when it was suggested to the Dalai Lama that Buddhism and Christianity are merely different traditions with the same fundamental beliefs, he retorted that such people as Zen-Christians are doing nothing more than trying "to put a yak's head on a sheep's body."[66]

In *Crossing the Threshold of Hope*, John Paul II has addressed the question of entertaining Zen practices as a supplemental avenue for Christian prayer or meditation:

> . . . it is not inappropriate to caution those Christians who enthusiastically welcome certain ideas originating in the religious traditions of the Far East—for example, techniques and methods of meditation and ascetical practice. In some quarters these have become fashionable, and are accepted rather uncritically.[67]

In order to provide clarity to those Catholic Christians who had become attracted, "uncritically," to the religious practices in Far Eastern traditions such as Buddhism, John Paul II recommended the "Letter to the Bishops of the Catholic Church on Some Aspects of Christian Meditation," written in 1989 by then Joseph Cardinal Ratzinger under the direction of the pope. The purpose of the document was to address the question of prayer "methods which are inspired by Hinduism and Buddhism, such as 'Zen,' 'Transcendental Meditation' or 'Yoga.'"[68] In this document, the Church cautions that:

> With the present diffusion of eastern methods of meditation in the Christian world and in ecclesial communities, we find ourselves faced with a pointed renewal of an attempt, which is not free from

65. Ricci, *True Meaning of the Lord of Heaven (T'ien-chu Shih-i)*, 395, 399.

66. Dalai Lama, *The Good Heart*, 105.

67. John Paul II, *Crossing the Threshold of Hope*, 89.

68. Ratzinger, "Letter to the Bishops of the Catholic Church on Some Aspects of Christian Meditation," Congregation for the Doctrine of the Faith, n. 1.

dangers and errors, 'to fuse Christian meditation with that which is non-Christian.'[69]

The principal difficulties that such practices as "Zen prayer" lead one into is the propensity to distort the purpose of Christian prayer, which is to worship and communicate with the transcendent God, and tends to abandon the "meditation on the salvific works accomplished in history by the God of the Old and New Covenant."[70]

Said another way, Zen, which was designed to attain to Buddhist ends, does not accord well with Christian prayer, which is designed to attain to Christian ends. Zen and Christianity point in different directions, and so do their methods of meditation. In the summary discussion of such "erroneous ways of praying," the Church's instruction on Eastern religious practices asserts that, "These and similar proposals to harmonize Christian meditation with eastern techniques need to have their contents and methods ever subjected to a thorough-going examination," so interested Christians can "avoid the danger of falling into syncretism."[71] When Bishop Frank Dewane discovered that yoga classes were being held during Eucharistic adoration in his diocese at St. Pope John XXIII Church—separated only by a glass partition—the concerned bishop was quick to order the yoga class cancelled.[72] Father Walter Kedjierski, an expert of Asian religion and culture and priest at St. Catherine of Siena Church in Franklin Square, New York, perhaps a bit acerbically asked:

> Have we chosen to abandon the richness of our own faith tradition for another? Have we sufficiently altered the ideas inherent in Zen and yoga about a total abandonment to all attachments and concepts that Christ and the truths of the faith can find a place in them? If the answer is No, then very clearly this is doing damage to the Catholic faith.[73]

69. Ibid., Part III, 12.

70. Ibid.

71. Ibid.

72. Flott, "When Worlds that Should Collide, Don't." Many Christians are unaware of yoga's essentially religious nature; the breathing and postures of yoga practice were created to enhance states of mental and spiritual "awareness" intended to lead to Hindu enlightenment. Yoga practice, according to Hinduism, involves the summoning of a *deva*, or spirit, that will act as the practitioner's guide.

73. Quoted in Flott, "When Worlds that Should Collide, Don't."

The words of Father Kedjierski, Pope John Paul II, and a number of Church documents convey to those who seek to mix Zen Buddhism and Catholicism an unambiguous message: Buddhist practice is an entryway into to Buddhist belief. Plainly said, Zen meditation is devised to facilitate one's realization of the "Buddha mind," and according the Zen practitioner there is no mind, no Buddha, and no Jesus.

Q: Why do I frequently hear of Buddhist retreats at Catholic locations?

It has become common for Catholic retreatants at monasteries, convents, retreat houses, and churches, to be offered Zen workshops or Buddhist meditation classes. Catholic sister, Sister Rose Mary Dougherty, SSND, is a Zen teacher who conducts meditation retreats, and is a sensei, or "teacher," in the lineage of the White Plum Buddhist samgha. When asked if leading Buddhist meditation classes clashes with Catholicism, Dougherty suggests that there are no conflicts between the two religions.[74] The Holy Family Passionist Retreat Center at Hartford, Connecticut, sponsored a retreat titled, "Zen Spirit—Christian Spirit: Meditation as a Christian Contemplative Practice." St. Joseph's Catholic Church in Richardson, Texas, held a Zen retreat in the church sanctuary, and the Benedictine sisters at Benet Hill Monastery in Colorado Springs, Colorado, feature a "Zen Garden" at their retreat center. Catholic priests and sisters regularly visit the Hsi Lai Buddhist Temple at Hacienda Heights, California, and the director of the Rochester Institute of Technology Catholic Campus Ministry, Father Richard Hunt, SJ, identifies himself with, among other things, Buddhism, Reiki healing, Tibetan Buddhist and Chinese healing arts, esoteric and psychic hands, and is a trained shaman healer.

One finds few retreats at these centers that offer more conventional Catholic practices, such as the Spiritual Exercises of Saint Ignatius, devotions to the Sacred or Immaculate Hearts, organized recitations of the rosary or various chaplets, frequent exposition of the Blessed Sacrament, or even the hallowed Benedictine practice of *lectio divina*, or "spiritual reading" centered on Holy Scripture, the works of the Church Fathers, or biographies of the saints. It is often asked why some Catholic retreat centers seem to avoid practices that are historically Catholic. To answer this question we

74. See http://www.religionnews.com/index.php?/rnstext/can_a_bishop_also_be_a_buddhist.

must first acknowledge that non-Catholic practices at retreat centers, such as Buddhist meditation, are usually offered with good intentions; it is often hoped that by offering a course on Zen meditation Catholics will deepen their relationship with God. This is admirable, and any Christian retreat should indeed be focused on this purpose. In many cases retreat organizers hope that more "progressive" spiritual practices will attract young people to what seems like a shrinking Church. They often hope that Buddhist meditation will offer an effective way to nourish spiritual growth and oppose the attraction of materialism.

I must admit, however, that perceived "explorative spriritualities" such as Zen Buddhism have become popular for no better reason than that they are popular. Retreatants who have participated in Zen workshops at Catholic venues often cite official Church documents to justify their practice, carefully selecting passages that appear to support their aims. Jesuit Law professor at Georgetown University, Father Robert Drinan, SJ, wrote that:

> *Dominus Iesus* (August 6, 2000) affirms that "inter-religious [dialogue], which is part of the Church evangelizing mission, requires an attitude of understanding and a relationship of mutual knowledge and reciprocal enrichment." . . . I found the "reciprocal enrichment" of this retreat particularly satisfying.[75]

Drinan continues to recall that, "I first experienced this spell of Buddhism in 1969 when I arrived in Vietnam with a human-rights team," and he notes that after attending the Zen retreat—where they chanted the *sutras* together during the workshop—he discovered that "Buddhist prayers are powerful." What he neglects to mention in his quotation of *Dominus Iesus*, is that "reciprocal enrichment" should only occur "in obedience to the truth," a concept that Zen Buddhism theoretically and practically rejects.[76] The same Vatican document quoted by Drinan also asserts that, "The Church's constant missionary proclamation is endangered today by relativistic theories which seek to justify religious pluralism."[77] Selective quotation from Church documents has become a cottage industry among some Catholic Christians.

The attempt to integrate Buddhism into Catholic retreats has inspired a number of new publications in the vein of Robert Kennedy's *Zen*

75. See Fr Robert Drinan, SJ, "A Zen Retreat," http://kennedyzen.tripod.com/retreat_drinan.htm. Accessed February 28, 2013.

76. *Dominus Iesus*, 2.

77. Ibid., 4.

Spirit—Christian Spirit. One book popularly sold at Catholic retreat centers, in addition to works by the Dalai Lama, is Carrin Dunne's *Buddha and Jesus: Conversations.* The book begins with a question to the reader:

> Have you ever brought together two people both of whom you loved dearly but who were previously unknown to each other? You probably had the feeling that were they to meet they would become fast friends, that they would find the same joy in each other that you find in each of them. . . .[78]

Of course, the "friends" Dunne's book introduces to each other are "Jesus of Nazareth" and "Siddhartha Gotama," and she continues by stating that, "At a certain level the dialogues are conversations between my inner Jesus and my inner Gotama."[79] Significantly, by the end of the book it is Jesus who becomes enlightened by the teachings of the Buddha.[80]

While "progressive spiritualities" may be appealing in a world of religious disagreement, and while religious pluralism seems to erase the religious boundaries that contribute to conflict, Zen retreats at Catholic churches and retreat centers neither represent truth, nor do they accurately and appropriately reflect what Catholicism teaches regarding how Christians should properly engage non-Catholic religions. Some Catholic retreat centers have justified their explorational use of Buddhist, or "Zen," meditation by claiming that they are following the so-called "spirit" of the Second Vatican Council, or that "borrowing" from Eastern religious practices is somehow "ecumenical," but these assertions largely misrepresent the Council's objectives. When Pope John XXIII envisioned the ecumenical dimension of the Council, he clearly and consistently stated that the Church's overtures to non-Christian or non-Catholic religions should serve as a "gentle invitation to seek and find that unity for which Jesus Christ prayed so ardently to his heavenly Father."[81] That is, ecumenism was not to change or compromise the Catholic faith, but rather to lovingly, and with open arms, welcome all persons into the Truth of Christ and into full communion with the Holy See.

A growing number of Catholic retreat centers are now responding to the last few decades of questionable "Zen" retreats by returning to the Church's long and rich history of traditional spiritual practices.

78. Dunne, *Buddha and Jesus,* 5.

79. Ibid.

80. Ibid., 97–98.

81. John XIII, *Ad Petri Cathedram,* 62.

The Gilmary, which means "servant of Mary," Catholic Retreat Center in Coraopolis, Pennsylvania, has featured retreat and lecture topics such as, "The Spiritual Exercises of Saint Ignatius Loyola," as well as events to help Catholic Christians participate in movements inaugurated by Pope Benedict XVI and Pope Francis. The Center's retreat on the traditional Spiritual Exercises of Saint Ignatius are led by the priests of Miles Christi, a young order dedicated to the spiritual direction of souls, and committed to the authentic teachings of the Church. Recent retreats at the San Pedro Center in Winter Park, Florida, have focused on the lives and spiritualities of popular saints, such as a retreat entitled, "A Taste of the Tradition: Teresa of Avila," and another called, "A Taste of the Tradition: Blessed John Henry Cardinal Newman." This Center has also offered programs on Church history and the meaning of Holy Week. And as priests become more aware of the Church's cautions against mixing Buddhism with Christianity, many have begun to organize Catholic retreats at their parishes based upon practices more in continuity with the perennial teachings of the Church. Several Catholic churches now offer the Benedictine meditative practice of *lectio divina*, for example, making the words of Scripture, rather than Buddhist methods of attaining *nirvana*, the focus of contemplation.

To reaffirm what I have already suggested, the Catholic Church does not claim that Buddhist meditation techniques are "evil," but it does strongly caution against the misconception that Buddhist ideas and meditative practices are, without qualification, compatible with Catholic belief and methods of prayer. While it may seem that through Eastern meditation one may achieve spiritual understanding, it is incorrect to assume that the Church does not already have similar, and perhaps more effective techniques for spiritual prayer and insight. Mother Teresa, who lived and served in India, the birthplace of Buddhism, once said that, "God speaks in the silence of the heart. Listening is the beginning of prayer." Her point is an important one; silence helps us better hear the voice of God. But Buddhist silence was not designed to hear the voice of God, for to a Buddhist, it can be argued, there is no God to hear.

SECTION TWO

Essential Beliefs Compared

Q: Is there a monotheistic, personal God in Buddhist teachings?

The first thing to know about this question is that Buddhists do not consider it an important question. Edward Conze accurately answers the problem of whether Buddhism believes in a monotheistic God in his statement that:

> Buddhist tradition does not exactly deny the existence of a creator, but it is not really interested to know who created the Universe. The purpose of Buddhist doctrine is to release beings from suffering, and speculations concerning the origin of the Universe are held to be immaterial to that task. They are not only a waste of time but may also postpone deliverance from suffering. . . . [1]

One of the hallmarks of Buddhism is its rejection of the question of existential origin asked within the Vedic texts that predated the Buddha. Simply said, Buddhism does not wonder about the origin of the universe or the existence of a monotheistic God because it is irrelevant to the goal of *nirvana*, and even more, the presence or absence of a God poses a problem to one of Buddhism's fundamental beliefs, that of non-duality.

The Buddhist understanding of non-duality holds that such dichotomies as creator and creation or God and man are false ideas imagined by human consciousness. In a rather complex Buddhist text called the *Satasahasrika*, the Buddha answers a question given by his disciple, Subhuti, "Where do duality and non-duality come about?" The Buddha answers

1. Conze, *Buddhism*, 39.

46

that, "Where there is no eye and forms, ear and sounds . . . no mind and dharmas, no enlightenment and non-enlightenment, that is non-duality."[2] In other words, Buddhism teaches that there are no actual dualities, and thus the idea of a God set apart from humans is rejected as an imagined pair; this idea is also expressed in the Buddha's teaching that there is no permanent self. In *The Heart Sutra*, which describes the enlightenment of Buddhism's famous bodhisattva ("enlightenment being"), Avalokitesvara (or Guanyin in China), the constituent parts of self are categorically denied to exist. The *sutra* expresses non-duality, or *shunyata* ("emptiness"), and non-self in this way: "In emptiness there is no form, nor feeling, nor perception, nor impulse, nor consciousness; no eye, ear, nose, tongue, body, mind; no forms, no sound, smells, tastes, touchables or objects of mind."[3] How can there be a personal God without first there being a person, or self, which Buddhism fundamentally disclaims.

This leads to the Buddhist response to the Christian attachment to Jesus Christ. In D. T. Suzuki's famous *Mysticism: Christian and Buddhist*, he recalled that, "Whenever I see a crucified figure of Christ, I cannot help thinking of the gap that lies between Christianity and Buddhism," a gap that represents "the psychological division separating the East from the West."[4] Whereas the notion of a self, or "individual ego," asserts itself in the West, Suzuki contends that according to the Buddhist way of thinking there is no belief in a permanent self. Jesus Christ as God incarnate makes little sense from the Buddhist point of view; indeed, Suzuki states that, "The ego (self) is non-existent and, therefore, there is no ego to be crucified."[5] What he is saying here is that since Buddhism does not accept the presence of an enduring self, there was no Jesus "self" to be crucified.

Suzuki continues to note that, "What is needed in Buddhism is enlightenment, neither crucifixion nor resurrection. A resurrection is dramatic and human enough, but there is still the odor of the body in it."[6] If there is no self, no other, and no dualities, there can obviously be no creator God to set in relationship with his creation. But in the end, it is impossible to assert that Buddhism denies the existence of God because it does not matter to Buddhism whether or not there is one. Edward Conze

2. Quoted in Conze, *Buddhist Texts Through the Ages*, 174.

3. In Conze, *Buddhist Scriptures*, 163.

4. Suzuki, *Mysticism*, 98.

5. Ibid.

6. Ibid., 101.

has addressed this conundrum: "If indifference to a personal creator of the Universe is atheism, then Buddhism is indeed atheistic."[7] D. T. Suzuki himself asserts that Zen is "not a religion in the sense that the term is popularly understood; for Zen has no God to worship."[8]

While Buddhism maintains that Christianity persists in its notion of a creator God paired with his creation, Christianity maintains that Buddhism persists in its denial of this truth. Whereas some Catholics choose to begin dialogue with areas of agreement, and indeed Christians and Buddhists do agree in significant areas, it is more fruitful to commence from the question of whether there is a monotheistic God, for Christianity rests entirely on the belief that there is. Christian belief in the One God derives from God's revelation to the people of Israel in the Hebrew "Shema Yisrael," Deuteronomy 6:4, "Hear, O Israel: the Lord our God, the Lord is one." This text, which dates to around 600 BC, and thus precedes the life of the historic Buddha, is a clear scriptural assertion that there is a single God, the very God we see creating the universe and humanity in Genesis. When Moses returned and presented the Ten Commandments to the people of Israel, the second of those commandments demanded that, "You shall have no other gods before me" (Exod 20:3). Judaic and Christian thinkers have spilled much ink demonstrating how faith in a creator God can be arrived at through reason, but it suffices to say that monotheism is a non-negotiable, *the* non-negotiable, assertion upon which Christianity bases everything else.

One of the main difficulties of dialogue between Catholics and Buddhists revolves around the "God question," since Buddhism can confidently assert its non-denial of the Christian God. The "God question" bears little relevance to the Buddhist aim to eliminate suffering, so it can be shrewdly evaded by Buddhist interlocutors; why does the existence of a God matter, they might ask. In a discussion of Christian-Buddhist differences, the theologian, Fritz Buri, states that Jesus, unlike the Buddha:

> . . . sees human existence within the history of God and his creation, which has a beginning and an end and which is determined by the struggle of God against powers having fallen from and now in opposition to him.[9]

7. Conze, *Buddhism*, 39.

8. Suzuki, *Introduction to Zen Buddhism*, 39.

9. Buri, "Comparison of Buddhism and Christianity," 16.

As Buddhism can avoid the question of whether there is a supreme God, Christians cannot. According to Christianity, human suffering can only be explained if one understands how "God and his creation" are presently in antagonism with fallen powers. Suffering can only properly be understood and relinquished in light of one's relationship to God and an understanding of where suffering comes from. Humanity cannot by itself eliminate suffering; God is the ultimate liberator of human anguish. Put another way, one is better prepared to call on God to help him if in the first place he believes God to exist.

Finally, whereas Christianity often speaks of God as a "Prime Mover," the "unmoved mover of all," Buddhism sets aside the question of the universal origins.[10] Christianity understands the world as "brought into being" by a divine creator; Buddhism "imagines reality to be the cause of itself, with no God beyond it as its transcendent Creator."[11] As Ninian Smart describes the Buddhist notion of the universe, it is "composed of a vast swarm of short-lived events"; whereas Buddhists see an impermanent and vanishing cosmos, Christians see a created world, brought into being by a creator God, and destined for eternal fulfillment. Saint Thomas Aquinas's assertion that the existence of God is suggested in the formula, *ex nihilo nihil fit*, "nothing comes from nothing," is foreign to Buddhist thought, for the universe simply is. It is without a creator. It is merely a web that has no weaver.

Q: According to Buddhism, is the Buddha God?

I have confronted this question in a previous response, but there is still more to say about the Buddhist belief of who the Buddha was, and is now in human consciousness. Since Buddhists do not believe in a creator God, or entertain the possibility of God's existence, Buddhists clearly do not believe the Buddha to be God. I have discussed the Buddha of history above, and here I will briefly outline the Buddha of religious belief. In simple terms, I can describe the Buddha's "salvific" gift to humanity to be what he taught; Jesus' gift, on the other hand, was largely what he did. Rather than being viewed as God, or a god, the Buddha is believed to have been a man who attained *buddhatva*, or "Buddhahood." Buddhahood, sometimes called "Buddha-nature," is considered to be a universal property of

10. See Fredericks, *Buddhists and Christians*, 43.

11. Ibid.

absolute understanding. Buddhists, in fact, do not consider the historic Siddhartha Gautama to have been the only Buddha; he is one of many who have attained the understanding of Buddhahood. The Pali Buddhist Canon includes a list of twenty-eight Buddhas, and the Mahayana tradition professes many thousands of Buddhas throughout history. Most Buddhist sects commonly affirm that the next Buddha will be one named Maitreya, the "Buddha of the future."

The Buddha who was formerly the prince, Siddhartha Gautama, is the most commonly known Buddha in the West, and his teachings constitute the core ideas of the Buddhist community today. Many Buddhists, especially those in Asia, enthusiastically await the coming Maitreya Buddha, who will as Jan Nattier says, "usher in a 'golden age' for his followers."[12] This messianic Buddha represents a certain hope for the future, "a time when all human beings could once again enjoy the spiritual and physical environment most favorable to enlightenment and the release from worldly suffering."[13] He is understood as a manner of future "savior" who follows after Gautama, the previous "savior." The important point here is that all Buddhas, including Gautama or the future Maitreya Buddha, are persons who have attained Buddhahood; there is no Buddhist sense that any of these Buddhas is God, in the sense that a Christian understands the God of the Holy Trinity to be God.

In contrast to God, who is omniscient (all-knowing) and omnipresent (ever-present), Buddhahood is distinguished by evident spiritual attributes. A Buddha is not a creator, nor is he metaphysically distinct from other beings. As "awakened" beings, Buddhas have attained the Buddha-nature, which is purified of the "three poisons": desire, aversion, and ignorance. Therefore Buddhas are often called "supreme humans" in Buddhism because they have freed themselves from the cycle of rebirths (*samsara*), and no longer suffer as unawakened people do. The state of Buddhahood is individually achieved, without the intervention of a supreme and relational God; awakening is accomplished through one's own efforts and merits. Said another way, Buddhism does not teach dependency on a God to attain enlightenment; the Buddha has simply pointed the way and it is up to Buddhists to follow that way on their own. Jesus Christ saved man through his Passion and death, redeeming humanity from its sin; the Buddha taught his followers the way to Buddhahood, which is release from human suffering.

12. Nattier, "Meanings of the Maitreya Myth," 24.

13. Sponberg, "Introduction," in *Maitreya, The Future Buddha*, 2.

These two religious views are very different. While Christ's nature as God allowed his sacrifice to be redemptive, the Buddha's gift to humanity, his teaching, did not require him to be more than a human person.

Although Buddhism has no concept of a God who created and now rules the universe, it does have an elaborate cosmology, which includes a complex network of *devas*, or deities. Both the Buddha, Gautama, and all other Buddhas, are regarded as "awakened beings," and the myriad Buddhas along with the innumerable *devas* are all subject to birth, death, rebirth, and eventual extinction. Buddhas and *devas* are impermanent; God is eternal. In a final word, the Buddha was a teacher and not a god; when describing himself, the Buddha exclaimed to his disciple, "O Vakalli, whoever sees the Dharma (teachings), sees me (the Buddha)."[14]

Q: Does Buddhism believe in supernatural beings, such as angels?

Reincarnation is not the only belief that Buddhism inherited from Hinduism; it also adopted the Hindu belief in a pantheon of supernatural divinities called *devas*. Kenneth Ch'en notes that early Buddhists, being former Hindus, accepted the notion that good behavior (*karma*) in this life could result in being born in the next as a *deva*. Ch'en says that, "Buddhists soon worked out a whole hierarchy of such deities, adapted mainly from prevailing Indian religions and mythologies, and modified to suit the needs of Buddhists," and that as *devas* they enjoy "happiness because of their past meritorious deeds."[15] These deities were ranked into three categories; *devas* of the "world of sensual pleasures," *devas* of the "world of form," and *devas* "of the formless world."[16] Despite the Buddhist resistance to acknowledging personal existence, Buddhist texts commonly admit the existence of deities without question. They are viewed as real beings with superhuman powers that were, on the whole, subservient to the great Buddha during his post-awakening life.[17]

Not unlike how Christians understand angels, Buddhist *devas* can be either good or evil, and as Guiseppe Tucci notes of Tibetan Buddhism, "Many of these powers are hostile under certain circumstances, evil in

14. *Vakkali Sutta*, SN 22.87.

15. Ch'en, *Buddhism*, 100–101.

16. Ibid., 101.

17. Trainor, *Buddhism*, 122.

nature, but most behave in an ambiguous and inconstant manner."[18] Of all forms of Buddhism, perhaps Tibetan Buddhism includes the most active and rich tradition of *deva* worship, and unlike Christianity, Tibetan Buddhist rituals are performed to appease and control malevolent gods. While Christianity does not pacify evil spirits through ritual offerings, Tibetan Buddhist rites are often performed to prevent the deity from seeking revenge on human beings. Tibetan deities are separated into "white and good" or "black and evil," and white spirits are worshiped while black ones are placated. This system of deities, some helpful and some fearful, has resulted in traditional apotropaic practices intended to protect believers from harm and shield their homes from spiritual attacks. Perhaps the most commonly held Buddhist understanding of spiritual beings is related to the belief in the Six Realms of Being.

Most Buddhists organize the progression of reincarnation into six realms, illustrated in the Tibetan painting of the Wheel of Life, sometimes called a "map of *samsara* (rebirth)." The first and sixth realms contain humans and animals, but the remaining four realms are occupied by supernatural beings of varying types. The second realm is reserved for *devas*, usually, but not always, defined as benevolent spirits that enjoy the happiness of a heavenly paradise, though the downside of being a *deva* is that the pleasure associated with this realm results in continued attachment, which hinders final enlightenment. In reality, the only two desirable rebirths in Buddhism are the human and *deva* realms; the others are all unfavorable. The third realm includes demons, which are evil spirits dominated by insatiable craving and anger. The fourth realm consists of what are called *pretas*, or "hungry ghosts" that are reborn with "large stomachs and very small throats, so they suffer with an extreme inability to satisfy their unrelenting thirst and hunger."[19] The fifth realm is known as the most horrifying, and is often referred to as the hell realm; this is where a being guilty of negative *karma* is reborn to undergo various torments of purification. Catholic students of Buddhism are sometimes inclined to compare this realm to purgatory, but the Buddhist hell realm is but a lower stage in the *samsaric* cycle, and does not result in entrance into "heaven."

Perhaps the most popular assembly of Buddhist deities is the collected bodhisattvas. A bodhisattva is initially a person, any person, who promises to follow the "bodhisattva path," which is simply, as Peter Harvey

18. Tucci, *Religions of Tibet*, 171.

19. Trainor, *Buddhism*, 62.

puts it, "to strive for Buddhahood for its own sake, and for the sake of helping suffering beings."[20] The more revered form of bodhisattva, however,
is a being who has gone "beyond being reborn according to *karma*, and
becomes a 'Great Being' . . . a heavenly saviour being" who is "certain to
attain Buddhahood."[21] What makes bodhisattvas at this level popular
among Buddhists is that they are then able to function like patron saints
who can be invoked for special assistance. The most famous bodhisattva in
contemporary Buddhism is Avalokitesvara, who is the patron bodhisattva
of mercy and childbearing. Like Catholic patron saints, bodhisattvas are
represented in paintings and statues, which are hung on walls or placed on
shrine tables to remind believers of their examples and assistance, though
unlike Catholic saints and angels, bodhisattvas are not intercessors, since
they are not believed to dwell in the presence of a God, who is the true and
ultimate source of help.

At this point one might ask if Buddhists might regard the Christian
God as a *deva*; after all, God is a divine being. James Fredericks judiciously
remarks that "the Christian God," the God of the Old and New Testaments,
"cannot be considered a *deva*, or even the highest of *devas*," for Christianity's God is not a sentient being, but rather the creator of sentient beings.[22]
This does not mean, however, that God is the creator of *devas*, at least as
they are understood in Buddhist terms. Christianity indeed believes in invisible beings, but they are not necessarily the same beings envisioned by
Buddhists. Catholicism, in contrast to Buddhism, believes in another group
of beings commonly known as angels. Angels, from the Latin term *angelus*,
meaning "one sent," or "messenger," are, like Buddhists understand *devas* or
pretas to be, beings with superhuman powers, but unlike Buddhist deities,
there are no angels of the "world of sensual pleasures" or of "the world of
form." Angels are more like the third category of *devas*, those of the "formless world." Yet even so, they are conceived of as a very different nature.

As in most Christian-Buddhist comparisons, the most significant de-
partures between the two traditions revolve around the Christian belief in
an all-powerful creator God. While *devas* and other Buddhist deities were
mainly subservient to the Buddha, and all the other myriad Buddhas, angels are represented in Scripture as a community of spiritual (formless) beings that are intermediate between God and humanity. As the Psalms state,

20. Harvey, *Introduction to Buddhism*, 122.

21. Ibid., 124.

22. Fredericks, *Buddhists and Christians*, 33.

"You have made him (mankind) a little less than the angels" (Ps 8:6). Even more to the point, angels, like humans, were created by God.[23] According to Catholicism, angels, which are higher than men, yet like men created by God, perform four principle occupations, some of which might appear to overlap with the Buddhist view of *devas* and *pretas*. As their name suggests, angels principally act as messengers, but they also serve as attendants at God's throne in heaven, render their protection over all created souls, or assist God in his governance of the created world.

In Scripture, angels most often appear as appointed messengers of God's will to men; Jacob's vision of angels ascending and descending the ladder that connects heaven and earth is a good image of this angelic function (Gen 28:10–19). Perhaps the best example of this task appointed to angels, as told in Luke, was performed by the angel Gabriel—angels have names—who was sent by the Father to inform the Virgin Mary that she would conceive and become the mother of Jesus, the Son of God, marking his Incarnation:

> The angel answered, "The Holy Spirit will come on you, and the power of the Most High will overshadow you. So the holy one to be born will be called the Son of God. Even Elizabeth your relative is going to have a child in her old age, and she who was said to be unable to conceive is in her sixth month. For no word from God will ever fail." "I am the Lord's servant," Mary answered. "May your word to me be fulfilled." Then the angel left her. (Luke 1:35–38)

In this example, not only is the angel Gabriel seen as a messenger of God, but Mary also serves as an example of humble obedience to God's message.

In the book of Daniel, we see the second duty of what the Catholic Church has traditionally called the "angelic hosts"; they are viewed as attendants upon God's throne in the court of heaven. Daniel describes the hosts in this way: "thousands of thousands ministered to him, and ten thousand times a hundred thousand stood before him: the judgment was set and the books were opened" (Dan 7:9–10). They often appear in Scripture "standing before God's throne," and remain by him to render their assistance whenever required.[24] Not only do they stand before God, but many angels additionally serve to guard and protect humans. Throughout Scripture Christians are reminded that God assigns an angel to each individual soul, and as Jesus said, "See that you despise not one of these little ones; for I say

23. See Psalms 148:2–5, Colossians 1:16–17.
24. See Tobit 12:15, or Revelation 8:2–5.

to you that their angels in Heaven always see the face of My Father Who is in Heaven" (Matt 18:10). According to Catholic belief, the fact that God has assigned a protective angel to each soul reveals the dignity attached to each human person. Saint Jerome once wrote: "how great the dignity of the soul, since each one has from his birth an angel commissioned to guard it."[25]

Not only do angels watch over all persons, but they also serve as divine agents who help God govern the world. Angels keep charge over regions assigned to them, and appear in the Bible performing acts on earth. An angel caused the plague that overcame Israel because of David's sin, and God intervened and stopped the angel from finally destroying Jerusalem: "And when the angel of the Lord had stretched out his hand over Jerusalem to destroy it, the Lord had pity on the affliction, and said to the angel that slew the people, 'It is enough'" (2 Sam 24:16). Angels who are charged with specific territories influence natural events in that area when called by God to do so, and some even cause lighter things to occur, such as wind that rustles trees (2 Sam 5:23–24). Buddhists believe that some deities, like angels, similarly watch over appointed regions, such as the so-called *catumaharajika devas*, who guard the four quarters of the earth. But Buddhist deities—as they are understood—are not subject to the commands of a single God, are not immortal like angels, and rarely intervene in human affairs.

Finally, both Catholics and Buddhists believe that there are both good and evil supernatural beings, though even this belief is different. A Christian does not, as in Tibetan Buddhism, placate evil angels, or demons, by giving them gifts. Scripture constantly refers to good and evil angels. The fall of the First Parents, for example, alludes powerfully to the presence of a "principle evil" that was jealous of Adam and Eve.[26] The fall of Lucifer, or Satan, is perhaps the most famous example of an angel who became evil, and we see him afflicting Job, with God's permission, with terrible sufferings; and Satan is called the "adversary" in Zechariah, when he entreats the Lord against Joshua the High Priest (Zech 3:1–3).

The Buddhist so-called equivalent of the fallen angel, Satan, is Mara, whose name appropriately means "death maker." Ninian Smart explains that under Mara's spell, "you will die and die and die again," and "rebirth," Smart notes, "is after all just a more optimistic name for the process of redeath."[27] Christians and Buddhists would agree that death is evil, and

---

25. Herbermann, *The Catholic Encyclopedia*, vol. 7, 49.

26. See Genesis 3.

27. Smart, *Buddhism and Christianity*, 19.

whether it is Satan or Mara who cause the process of death, both religions concur that these supernatural beings are "bad." But Mara also indirectly causes rebirth—life—and Christians value life as holy; Buddhists hold that life causes death (negative), whereas Christians hold that death precedes eternal life (positive), given that death occurs in God's grace. The important thing to remember is that while Buddhist deities are independent agents who are ultimately not accountable to a Buddha or a god, angels, as understood by Christians, are ultimately powerless before God. And in addition, even when Buddhist deities and Christian angels appear to be alike, such as Mara and Satan, their similarities are only superficial, and diminish when their essential natures are better understood.

To offer what is perhaps a trite example of the differences I am suggesting, we might consider an example of a short prayer many Catholic children are taught when growing up, a "Prayer to one's Guardian Angel" that is traditionally prayed at one's bedside before sleep:

> Angel of God, my guardian dear,
> to whom God's love commits me here.
> Ever this night be at my side,
> to light and guard, to rule and guide. Amen.

Such a prayer would not be found within Buddhism precisely because there is no God in Buddhism, whose love commits *devas* to souls, "to light and guard, to rule and to guide."

Q: According to Buddhism, where did the world come from? According to Christianity, where did the world come from?

This is perhaps one of the most common questions Westerners ask about Buddhism, and the answer generally does not satisfy inquirers. For Buddhists, the question of where the universe came from is unimportant, and is ultimately irrelevant to the goal of enlightenment. It surprises many Catholics to learn that, for the most part, East Asian society has not considered the important issue of creation, and in fact, as Frederick Mote states, China, for example, regards "the world and man as uncreated, as constituting the central features of a spontaneously self-generating cosmos having no creator, no god, ultimate cause or will external to itself."[28] A society and

28. Mote, *Intellectual Foundations*, 18.

religion without a god or creator is almost unimaginable to most Catholic Christians, but this is precisely the position held by Buddhists and indeed most Asian philosophical and religious traditions. While creation *ex nihilo*, or "out of nothing," is a distant concept to Buddhism, it does consider the origin of things from another angle, that of what is often called "dependent co-arising." Simply said, this doctrine holds that things arise from causality, and not from creation.

In Leo Lefebure's book comparing Christianity and Buddhism, *The Buddha and the Christ*, Lefebure writes:

> For Buddhists, dependent co-arising is the web of mutual inter-relationships that binds all beings into a whole and makes them one. . . . All things are what they are, arising from the other things in the universe. Nothing arises from nothing, and so there is no question of a Creator calling things to be out of nothing.[29]

In one Buddhist text, the second-century BC sage, Nagasena, informs King Menander that, "there are not any things that exist which come out of things that did not exist. Only out of things that existed, great king, come things that exist."[30] The Buddhist view directly opposes Thomas Aquinas's argument that God indeed creates "from nothing."

One way to envision the Buddhist understanding of the universe is to imagine, as I have said above, a web that has no weaver; every action that occurs on a web can be felt, and affects all other parts of the web, but the question of where the web came from is inconsequential. The closest thing to a Buddhist cosmology, or "universe," is the Six Realms, which represents above all the cycle of rebirths that all sentient beings are believed to exist within. Tibetan Buddhism, however, adopted a creation account from Tibet's ancient Bon folk religion, which has been grafted onto the traditional understanding of the Six Realms that exist independent of a creator. Tibetan Buddhists thus speak of an original god of the cosmos "who existed when there was neither sun nor moon, nor time, nor the seasons, but only pure potentiality," a god that created beings from light and darkness.[31] But despite this creation myth, which is taken from a Tibetan folk religion probably influenced by earlier Iranian beliefs, advanced Tibetan Buddhist teachers consider this creation myth more didactic than actual. The story functions to teach good behavior rather than to explain the origin of the

---

29. Lefebure, *Buddha and the Christ*, 47.

30. Quoted in Stryk, *World of the Buddha*, 102.

31. Tucci, *The Religions of Tibet*, 214.

universe, for good *karma* results from acting like the beings of light, rather than those created from the darkness. In the end, even Tibetan Buddhists perceive the cosmos as a web without a weaver.

To ask where the world came from according to Buddhism is a moot question, for according to Buddhism the question is irrelevant to the real point of religious attainment, which is to end all suffering. What matters to Buddhists is the positive or negative *karma* produced by present actions, rather than the origin of all previous actions. Summarizing the Buddhist response to creation myths, Peter Harvey states:

> Buddhism sees no need for a creator of the world, as it postulates no ultimate beginning of the world, and regards it as sustained by natural laws. Moreover, if there were a creator of the world, he would be regarded as responsible for all the suffering which is found throughout it.[32]

In other words, Buddhism not only discards creation as an irrelevant question, but since all existing beings are believed to suffer, Buddhists question why a god might create beings into suffering. For Catholic Christians, however, the question of creation cannot be ignored, because if there is indeed a creator God, then everything must be viewed in light of God's design and will, and furthermore, the notion of an all-good God who creates beings with free will has not been traditionally considered by the Buddhist samgha. Within Buddhism there is simply no God, no creation, and no reason to consider cosmological origins.

For Christians, it is God who has brought the substance of all things into existence from a state of non-existence, or as it is expressed in the technical Latin language of the Church, *productio totius substantiâ ex nihilo sui et subjecti.* The crucial difference between Christianity and Buddhism is that Christians believe in a God, who was uncreated, and who can—and has—created things from nothing (*ex nihilo sui*); God did not originally transform what was already present, but rather creates, as it were, from nothing. While the Catholic understanding and interpretation of the Bible's picturesque account of God's creation of the universe and humanity is too involved to recount here, it will suffice to say that the Church believes and professes that the same God of the Old Testament, Elohim or Yahweh, created the world and man, as is theologically described in the first two chapters in Genesis.

---

32. Harvey, *Introduction to Buddhism,* 36.

Even more to the point of the comparison is the nature of God as understood by Christians, for when God said to Moses, "I Am That I Am: and he said, Thus shall you say to the children of Israel, I Am has sent me to you," Christians understand that God is "underived." He is not, as Buddhism claims all things are, derived from a previous action. Furthermore, Christians understand God, as the creator of all things, to be superior to his creation. "For the whole world before you is as the least grain of the balance," states the Bible, "and as a drop of the morning dew, that falls down upon the earth" (Wis 11:23). God is the beginning and end of all things; "I am he; I am the first and I am the last" (Isa 48:12). In confirmation of the Old Testament assertions regarding God as the creator of all things, Saint Paul wrote in his letter to the Romans, "For from him and through him and for him are all things. To him be the glory forever! Amen" (Rom 11:36). And as if these passages are not enough to support the biblical assertion that the God of Israel is viewed by his followers to be the creator of all, Isaiah includes this important affirmation: "I am the Lord, the Maker of all things, who stretches out the heavens, who spreads out the earth by myself" (Isa 44:24).

It should be clear by now that Christians understand God to be the "first cause," a creator without himself being created. The Buddhist understanding, in contrast, denies this assumption. In his consideration of Buddhist views of "creation and creator," José Ignacio Cabezón, writes that the Buddhist intellectual:

> . . . repudiates the notion that the universe as a whole (the totality or collection of all the world systems) has a first cause. Although they believe that any one world system goes through a process of creation and destruction, they share the view that the universe as a whole extends infinitely back in time. Put another way, there is no point before which there was nothing. Because there is no absolute origin, there is no first cause, and it follows, of course, that no one being (for example, God) could therefore have been that first cause.[33]

There are two very different beliefs expressed here; while Christians believe God, the "first cause," to have created all things out of his love for man, Buddhists believe that all material things have always existed in some form, and that there has been an eternal regression of causes that extends into an eternal past.

33. Cabezón, "Three Buddhist Views of the Doctrines of Creation and Creator, 34.

From the Christian view, only a clear understanding of God's role as creator can prevent having a distorted view of humanity's role in the cosmos. Emperor Constantine's advisor and tutor to his son, Lactantius, a Christian, was able to summarize the correct hierarchy of God's creation, and articulate plainly God's vision of his design:

> The world was made that we might be born. We were born that we might know God. We know Him that we may worship Him. We worship Him that we may earn immortality. We are rewarded with immortality that, being like unto the angels, we may serve Our Father and Lord forever, and be the eternal kingdom of God.[34]

Q: Who did Jesus and the Buddha say they were?

It is when discussing how Jesus and Buddha described themselves that we see Christianity and Buddhism again radically depart. As we consider who the Buddha said he was, we first recall that there is more than one Buddha according to Buddhism. Reacting to the statement in the Apostle's Creed, "I believe in Jesus Christ," the prolific Buddhist writer, Thich Nhat Hanh, wrote that, "In the tradition of Buddhism, the Buddha is not unique because there are so many Buddhas, countless Buddhas of the past, of the present, and of the future."[35] It is easy to understand how this statement can be made in light of the fact that a Buddha is simply an "awakened one," and the Buddha most Westerners imagine is the historic Siddhartha Gautama, who, as stated above, was but one of many awakened ones. So, who did the Gautama Buddha say he was?

When referring to himself in sermons and discussions, the Buddha identifies himself as Tathagata, which has a rather paradoxical meaning. In Buddhist *sutras*, the Buddha prefers to call himself Tathagata rather than use the pronouns "I" or "me," which is because of the Buddhist doctrine of no-self. It would make little sense for the Buddha to speak in the first person in light of his insistence that he had no constant self to refer to. Tathagata ironically means two things simultaneously, "one who has thus come" and "one who has thus gone," which implies that the Buddha is beyond all coming and going. Or more accurately said, he is no longer trapped

34. Lactantius, *Divinarum Institutionum*, VI, vi. For the complete version of this important text, see Lactantius, *Divine Institutes*, Anthony Bowen and Peter Garnsey, trans. (Liverpool: Liverpool University Press, 2003), 404.

35. Thich Nhat Hanh, *Going Home*, 137.

within the cycle of rebirth. The Buddha viewed himself as no longer having a distinct, *karma*-causing self, and his last words to this effect are recorded in the *Parinirvana Sutra*, or "scripture on the final extinction."

The setting of the *Parinirvana Sutra* is the moment of the Buddha's final death, after which he will no longer be reborn into one of the Six Realms. In a first-century biography of the Buddha's life called the *Buddha-carita*, or "Acts of the Buddha," the Indian poet, Ashcaghosa, recounts that when the Buddha at last reclined himself to experience his final extinction, he said to his disciples, "Everything comes to an end, though it may last for an aeon. The hour of parting is bound to come to an end."[36] And after leaving a few final exhortations, the Buddha disappeared into oblivion. The *Buddhacarita* records his last actions and the *Parinirvana Sutra* records his final teachings. Unlike Jesus, who promised to return, and in the meantime to remain with his disciples, guiding them in the Holy Spirit, the Buddha left nothing behind but what he had taught his followers. The Buddha announced before dying that, "The Doctrine and Discipline . . . which I have taught and enjoined upon you is to be your teacher when I am gone," and finally he instructed his disciples to, "work out your salvation with diligence," that is, on their own.[37] What the Buddha left behind after his death is his body of teachings. He nowhere professes to be divine or to leave behind him a spiritual guide or leader to assure that his teachings are correctly interpreted and transmitted.

The Buddha's teachings took on significant value to later Buddhists, and the Buddha himself claimed that his greatest legacy was his Dharma, or teachings, which would help human beings escape suffering by escaping attachments, especially an attachment to self-permanence. In one celebrated passage, the Buddha compares himself and his Dharma to a rain cloud:

> The Tathagata am I . . . arisen in the world just like a rain cloud.
> I shall refresh all living beings, whose bodies are withering away,
> who cling to the triple world [thinking, feeling, and action], who
> whither away in pain. . . . Setting aside all tiredness, I rain the rain
> of the Dharma.[38]

---

36. Quoted in Conze, *Buddhist Scriptures*, 63. Another irony I might point out here is that while Buddhism rejects the possibility of a creative beginning, "from nothing," the Buddha here speaks of the ultimate "end" of all things.

37. Quoted in Warren, *Buddhism in Translations*, 107 and 109.

38. Quoted in Conze, *Buddhist Texts Through the Ages*, 139–140.

The Dharma is of such central importance in Buddhism that Buddhists often refer to the "two bodies" of Buddhism: the "Buddha body," represented by the physical body of the Buddha before his final extinction, and the "Dharma body," which remains to instruct human beings in how to escape suffering and attain *nirvana*.

While it may be tempting to make authoritative comparisons of similarity between the Buddha and Jesus Christ, such comparisons eventually fall short, no matter the good intentions behind them. Looking at Jesus from a Buddhist perspective the Dalai Lama asserted that he views Jesus Christ as "either a fully enlightened being or a bodhisattva of a very high spiritual realization."[39] Despite the Dalai Lama's esteem for Jesus Christ, this is not who Jesus, himself, said he was. Ninian Smart has cogently responded to such comparisons by reminding us how differently each figure viewed his role in the "salvation" of human beings:

> Jesus saved humanity through his deeds and death—he was a sacrifice which restored the breach between human beings and the Divine, and the way of the Cross, however unlooked for, was nevertheless the path that the salvific plan of action took. The Buddha saves through his teaching above all.[40]

Not only did each man describe himself differently in terms of his own divinity or lack of divinity, but each also had very different ideas of what salvation means. Christ, who identified himself as both God and human, reconciled humanity, who lives only once and has an eternal soul, to a divine God; but the Buddha identified himself as the bearer of a special teaching, or Dharma, that helps humanity, who lives through countless rebirths, and finally ends his suffering by *nirvana*, or the final extinction of the self.

Before I outline who Jesus unambiguously said he was, it serves to reiterate that the Buddha preferred to leave his own identity ambiguous, if not even to suggest that anyone who wished to "know who the Buddha is" will never be able to do so. In the *Vajracchedika Sutra*, or "Diamond Cutter Sutra," the disciple Subhuti asked the Buddha to more clearly identify himself: "Whereupon the World-Honored One uttered this verse: 'Who sees my form, who seeks me in sound, perverted are his footsteps upon the way; for he cannot perceive the Tathagata.'"[41] Quite the opposite of exhorting his followers to "seek their salvation on their own," and that seeking him is

39. Dalai Lama, *The Good Heart*, 83.

40. Smart, *Buddhism and Christianity*, 13.

41. In Price and Wong Mou-lam, *The Diamond Sutra & the Sutra of Hui-neng*, 47.

to seek a false illusion, Jesus said, "Come to me all you who labor and are burdened, and I will refresh you" (Matt 11:28). Not only has he left behind the "sound" of his Word in Scripture, but as the insightful writer, Thomas à Kempis, has said, Jesus has left behind his tangible "form" in the Blessed Sacrament. Jesus, as God, has not abandoned his people. As à Kempis wrote in his *Imitation of Christ*, "O sweet and amiable word in the ear of a sinner, that Thou, O Lord my God, shouldst invite the poor and needy to the communion of Thy most sacred Body."[42] Not only is his "form" and "sound" still present in the world, but Jesus beckons all persons to both.

Despite the varied attempts by some secularists and religious seekers to de-divinize Jesus, to reimagine him, as the Dalai Lama does, as a "bodhisattva of a very high spiritual realization" or a benevolent guru, Jesus asserted his own divinity and authority quite clearly. In a dispute over the true identity of Jesus, he said to his interlocutors, "You are from below; I am from above. You are of this world; I am not of this world" (John 8:23). And shortly after this assertion of his status above created persons, he proclaimed, "Very truly I tell you . . . before Abraham was born, I am!" (John 8:58). Jesus could not have more directly identified himself as God, for this is how God identified himself in the Old Testament when Moses asked for his name during the Exodus (Exod 3:14).

Another difference between how the Buddha and Jesus identified themselves is seen when Jesus proclaimed himself to have dominion and authority over all of creation. Nearing his final hour, Jesus "looked toward heaven" and said:

> Father, the hour has come. Glorify your Son, that your Son may glorify you. For you granted him authority over all people that he might give eternal life to all those you have given him. Now this is eternal life: that they know you, the only true God, and Jesus Christ, whom you have sent. I have brought you glory on earth by finishing the work you gave me to do. And now, Father, glorify me in your presence with the glory I had with you before the world began. (John 17:1–5)

Not only does Jesus declare his sovereignty over "all people," but he also claims the power to give eternal life to his followers; both of these assertions are alien to the Buddha's definition of himself.

To overlook the times when Jesus defined himself as God, as king over all, and the "way, truth, and the life," as teacher, and even as judge, is

---

42. à Kempis, *My Imitation of Christ*, 383–84.

to misshape the central view of Jesus, of Christology, and of the Christian faith: There is one God, and the person of Jesus Christ as part of the Holy Trinity was incarnate in order to conquer death and redeem humanity from its sin. Scholars who struggle to make Jesus and the Buddha two "brothers" with the same message and with the same identity are falsifying what each person conveyed about himself. Scholars such as Seichi Yagi, who claim that there is "a depth where all oppositions [between Jesus and the Buddha] are overcome," have not yet deeply considered the implications of Jesus' assertions about who he was.[43] This "depth," Yagi claims, "is deeper than the Son of Man, the rule of God, 'Christ' or 'Amida Buddha' as Sambhogakaya. Jesus called it 'God,' Zen calls it 'the formless.'"[44] While such statements may appear beautifully written from the Buddhist or religious pluralist point of view, such assertions are arguably sophistic, for as much as one might like Jesus and the Buddha to not be in disagreement, who they were, and who they said they were, are not the same, and two contradictory assertions, according to the logic of the Catholic intellectual tradition, cannot both be true. The Jesus Christ of Christianity was, in fact, a revolutionary, for he was and told the truth, no matter the inconvenience. George Orwell, who was by no means a believing Christian, understood the difficulty of proclaiming truth to an interlocutor who has judged it inconvenient when he suggested that in a time of universal deceit, telling the truth is a revolutionary act.

Q: Did the Buddha perform miracles? Did Jesus perform miracles?

As common as miracles are in the Bible, they are equally common in early Buddhist texts, and if there is an area of comparative similarity between the Buddha and Jesus Christ, it is the number of miracles attributed to them. In fact, the apparent similarities of their miracles has led some to create inventive stories conflating the two men, and some writers have suggested even that miracles attributed to Jesus were originally Buddhist myths. Scholars of Buddhism, such as Guang Xin, divide the miracles associated with Siddhartha Gautama into two categories: "the supernormal events that occurred in nature to mark special occasions to mark the life of the Buddha, such as his birth, enlightenment and death," and "the supernormal

43. Seichi Yagi, "Paul and Shinren," 209.
44. Ibid.

acts performed by Gautama Buddha himself."[45] Among the most striking miracles attributed to Jesus and the Buddha fall into the first category, that is, the circumstances associated with their respective births. In the case of Jesus' birth, we read in Saint Matthew's gospel that, "When his mother Mary had been betrothed to Joseph, before they came together, she was found to be with child of the Holy Spirit" (Matt 1:18). Christ was miraculously conceived of a Virgin mother by the Holy Spirit, one part of the Holy Trinity.

Buddhist accounts of Siddhartha Gautama's birth are equally miraculous. Legend has it that the Buddha's mother, Shuddhodana, dreamed that a white elephant entered her right side and impregnated her.[46] At her conception several miracles are reported—the blind began to see, the lame began to walk, and the deaf began to hear—and while she was pregnant the child was visibly seen sitting cross-legged inside the womb, and was heard preaching by nearby people. The story continues that Shuddhodana gave birth to her son in a forest grove, that Siddhartha came out of her right side without the usual pains of childbirth, and that the baby was so pure that it was spotless as it emerged. The new infant immediately took seven steps to the north and exclaimed, "This is my last birth; there shall be to me no other state of existence. I am the greatest of all beings."[47] In addition to the various phenomena associated with his birth, the Buddha also is purported to have performed miracles during the years he taught in public.

Buddhist sources report that three weeks after his enlightenment the *devas* were still suspicious about whether he had truly attained *nirvana*, and so to convince them he created a golden bridge using only his mind, and then he walked over it for a week to demonstrate the command of his supernatural capabilities. According to this account, the Buddha returned to his home kingdom, where much like Jesus' experience, the people there did not believe him. So in order to prove the legitimacy of his awakening, or Buddhahood, he performed what is referred to as the "twin miracle," where he, as Narada Mahathera describes, made "water and fire issue from the pores of his body simultaneously."[48] The inventory of the Buddha's miracles has grown through the ages, ranging from controlling elephants to taming floodwaters, all of which have functioned to highlight his special

45. Guang Xin, *Concept of the Buddha*, 15–16.

46. For a longer account of this legend see Gupta, *Elephant In Indian Art and Mythology*, 31.

47. In Manmatha Nhat Shastri, *Buddha*, 5.

48. Narada Mahathera, *Buddha and His Teachings*, 199.

powers. Just as in Christian accounts of Jesus' miracles, Buddhist miracles continued to be recorded after the death of the Buddha.

Catholic pilgrimage sites such as Lourdes and Fatima are well-known places where miracles have attracted large numbers of Christian faithful, and Buddhist pilgrimage sites are no different. From the Buddhist perspective, however, one does not visit a pilgrimage site as an act of worship, penance, or to ask for assistance, as is common of Christian pilgrimage; Buddhist pilgrims normally make difficult journeys to pilgrimage sites to attain personal merit, which in turn earns them positive *karma* and brings them nearer enlightenment. As Susan Naquin and Yu Chun-fang put it, visiting Buddhist sacred sites, "is highly meritorious and helps one loosen one's bonds to this life."[49] But even so, pilgrims often report miracles connected to the sites they visit, and in China, Buddhists describe special visions and miraculous events bestowed to seekers. Certainly, Buddhism has a rich history of miracle stories, attached both to the Buddha himself and to later followers, but the question is whether the Buddha reportedly performed miracles as Jesus did, and the Buddhist answer is clearly yes, though Buddhists view miracles as the sign of an enlightened being instead of an all-powerful God.

I am unaware of any formal declarations by the Catholic Church regarding the authenticity of Buddhist miracles, but it is the constant teaching of the Christian faith that miracles are either performed by good powers, which function under the auspices of God, or bad powers, which function under the auspices of the Enemy. That God can work through other religious traditions is certainly up to him, but by and large the normative avenue through which God performs miracles was through his Son, during his time on earth, or through his followers who have been empowered by the Holy Spirit. While Protestant or Orthodox Christians may quibble over some of the post-Resurrection miracles recognized by the Catholic Church, such as those at Lourdes and Fatima, most Christians recognize that Jesus himself performed miracles during his public ministry, most notably his cures, exorcisms, control over nature, and the resurrection of the dead.

Among the differences between the miracles of Jesus and the stated miracles of the Buddha include the nature of the miracles performed. While it appears that the predominance of miracles attributed to the Buddha were intended to establish his power and unique place among humans, the majority of Jesus' miracles involved curing the afflicted. The gospels,

49. Naquin and Chun-fang Yu, *Pilgrims and Sacred Sites in China*, 4.

for example, contain several instances of Jesus curing the blind: He cured a blind man in Bethsaida (Mark 8:22–26); he healed the blind near Jericho shortly before his Passion;[50] and he cured two blind men in Galilee (Matt 9:27–31). The restoration of sight recounted in the Bible, at one level, alludes to the gift of faith, so important to Christianity, for when he cured the men of Galilee they knew him to be the "Son of David," the Messiah.

Jesus' miracles also embody Christ's appeal to his followers to perform acts of charity on behalf of others, not to earn "*karmic* merit" for oneself, but rather as an expression of unselfish love, to be "the hands and feet of Christ," as the Christian expression asserts. To encourage this point Jesus healed the "untouchables," the rejected and unwanted of society, the lepers. Saint Matthew recorded such a cure:

> And when he came down from the mountain, great multitudes followed him. And behold a leper came and adored him saying, "Lord, if you will it, you can make me clean." And Jesus stretched forth his hand, touched him, and said: "I will it, be made clean." And then his leprosy was cleansed. And Jesus said to him: "See that you tell no man, but go, show yourself to a priest and offer the gift which Moses commanded as a testament to them." (Matt 8:1–4)

In addition to lepers, Jesus healed paralytics, a hemorrhaging woman, a man with dropsy, a person with a withered hand, the deaf, and many others. He likewise performed exorcisms, also a form of healing, but perhaps most dramatic of his public miracles were his resurrections of the dead.

A "ruler of the synagogue named Jairus" implored Jesus to heal his daughter who was on the point of death, but on his way to the house he was informed that the girl had already died. When Jesus had arrived, he informed the people gathered that, "the girl is not dead, but merely asleep" (Mark 5:39). The people laughed at him and scorned him, but he sent them away, entered the girl's room, and said to her, "Arise"; she then arose from the dead and walked (Mark 5:41). He also resurrected a young man from Nain, and most famously, Lazarus, who had already been dead for four days before Jesus called him from his tomb.[51] While all of Christ's miracles function in large part to confirm his divinity, or to demonstrate what theologians call his "hypostatic union," being both God and man, there is an even stronger sense that they support his message of charity.

50. See all three of the Synoptic Gospels.
51. See Luke 7:11–17, and John 11:1–44.

There are today both Christians and Buddhists who downplay the historical veracity of the reported miracles of both Jesus and the Buddha in an attempt to disregard the more "superstitious" elements of these two traditions, though from the Catholic view it is a point of logic that if God is the creator of all, and if Jesus is God, then miracles are within his power; to deny his miracles is, in a very real sense, to question his divinity. Perhaps it is easier to ask whether the Buddha or Jesus were reputed to have performed miracles than it is to answer whether their miracles were only stories, or really took place; both traditions claim they actually performed the miracles attributed to them. Buddhist discourse in recent years has shifted somewhat away from the miraculous, however, and has grown more philosophical. One of the differences between Christians and Buddhists is the enduring Christian belief that Jesus actively performs miracles; Christians in our current secularized society continue to pray for miracles, and believe they are often granted.

Q: What is the Buddhist belief regarding sin and salvation? What is the Christian belief regarding sin and salvation?

The Christian use of the word "sin" does not accurately describe the Buddhist idea of wrong behavior, and even more to the point, the Catholic understanding of how sin relates to salvation is very different from what a Buddhist might imagine. This is so because the word "salvation," which is related to sin, also carries radically different meanings to Catholics and Buddhists. To begin with, while a Christian is rightly concerned that her or his sins have offended and separated her or him from a loving and all-powerful God, the Buddhist believes there is no God to be marginalized or separated from. The Buddhist is principally occupied with eliminating suffering rather than maintaining a right relationship with his creator. He will thus be more focused on whether his actions have produced good or bad *karma*, for only his own state of being ultimately matters when seeking final enlightenment, or Buddhist "salvation."

I have already defined *karma* as "action," but there is more to this Buddhist doctrine than the simple notion that one's actions have consequences, for according to Buddhism consequences transfer to multiple lifetimes. Keith Yandell and Harold Netland have explained the Buddhist implications of *karma* in this way:

> So when one's body dies, one still has consequences coming. Thus one must be reborn to receive these consequences. But then in this new lifetime one also performs actions and thereby initiates yet further consequences. The consequences again are not exhausted within one's current lifetime. So again one must die and be reborn in still different consequences. So it goes, forever, unless something radical happens to break the cycle.[52]

The closest thing in Buddhism to "sin," then, is an action that causes bad *karma*, or bad consequences.

In Buddhism there is only one's own *karma* to control; one way to distinguish the Christian from Buddhist ideas of sin is to define them as "violationist" and "consequentialist." A good example of how sin is described from a Christian point of view is the assertion of Saint John, that, "Everyone who commits sin is guilty of lawlessness; sin is lawlessness" (1 John 3:4). An entirely different way of imagining sin is expressed in Buddhist texts: "Whatever a man does, the same he in himself will find, the good man, good: and evil he that evil has designed; and our deeds are all like seeds, and bring forth fruit in kind."[53] In other words, Christian sin is seen as violating a law, while Buddhist sin is seen as planting seeds with bad consequences.

Catholic teaching holds that sin is intimately connected to the human need for salvation, so it is natural to ask if Buddhism also sees this connection. Just as "sin" can be defined in different ways, however, so too can the notion of "salvation," and when discussing salvation the logical question is, saved from what? Buddhists seek salvation from suffering, and the only way to escape suffering is to achieve *nirvana*, which literally means to "extinguish a flame." Buddhist salvation is thus *nirvana*, a state of no desire, wherein all attachments have been extinguished, as if the oxygen that feeds a flame, like the desires that feed suffering, is no longer present. One of the main problems Christians confront when attempting to make sense of *nirvana* is, if Buddhism denies a real self, then what "self" is there

---

52. Yandell and Netland, *Buddhism*, 119.

53. From the Pali Jataka, no. 222, quoted in Suzuki, *Outlines of Mahayana Buddhism*, 184.

to achieve *nirvana*? This may sound like an unusual question, but it is one that Buddhists themselves have asked for more than two millennia.

In his highly philosophical work, *Buddhism and Christianity: A Preface to Dialogue*, Georg Siegmund writes that, "The salvation proper to nirvana is achieved only by the person who passes beyond the plane of the profane world and gains access to the very different plane of the unconditioned."[54] Despite the common Western assumption that *nirvana* is a place of blissful repose, imagined to be much like the Christian idea of heaven, the key term in Siegmund's statement is "unconditioned," which suggests a state of non-causation. And for there to be non-causation there must be a state wherein nothing exists to produce actions and reactions. It is therefore incorrect to equate *nirvana* with a state of happiness, since there is actually nothing to experience that one imagines as pleasure. As Siegmund also says, *nirvana*, which is the Buddhist's goal, is explained as "absolute nothingness."[55] And according to Zen Buddhism, the way to achieve *nirvana*, or Buddhist salvation, is to realize that one is already enlightened; that is, we live under the illusion that we are not yet in *nirvana*. Another way to describe the Buddhist idea of "sin," then, is any action whatever, since action is the basic carrier of *karma*, which is in turn the fuel that perpetuates rebirth, or suffering.

Leo Lefebure has summarized the question of how sin and salvation in Buddhist and Christian teachings can be compared:

> On the one hand, one can caution that because Christians believe in God and Buddhists do not, any similarities between Buddhist and Christian language are superficial. It can be claimed that Buddhist enlightenment is an awakening from suffering to knowledge of who we already are; Christian salvation is a supernatural gift from God, who is both beyond anything we can imagine and closer to us than we are ourselves.[56]

If sin, imagined from a Buddhist point of view, is merely an action that produces bad *karmic* consequences, and if salvation means the extinction of self, or *nirvana*, what is the Catholic understanding of sin and salvation?

In the simplest terms, salvation according to Christianity is the liberation of the soul from sin and its effects, which is made possible by the life, death, and Resurrection of Jesus Christ. The *Catechism of the Catholic Church* puts it this way:

54. Siegmund, *Buddhism and Christianity*, 128.
55. Ibid., 126.
56. Lefebure, *Buddha and the Christ*, xxi.

> By his glorious Cross Christ has won salvation for all men. He redeemed them from the sin that held them in bondage. "For freedom Christ has set us free." In him we have communion with the "truth that makes us free." The Holy Spirit has been given to us and, as the Apostle teaches, "Where the Spirit of the Lord is, there is freedom." Already we glory in the "liberty of the children of God."[57]

What one immediately discerns from the Church's description of salvation is how Chistocentric its understanding is. There can be no salvation without Jesus Christ and his redemptive death on the Cross. And as Saint Paul very plainly states, "if you confess with your mouth, 'Jesus is Lord,' and believe in your heart that God raised him from the dead, you will be saved" (Rom 10:9).

Far from the Buddhist notion that salvation is the cessation of all suffering, which is caused by all actions, the Church believes, rather, that it is precisely through the salvific action of Jesus on the Cross, the good and holy actions of human persons, and especially through faith, which is itself an action, that human persons are saved. Instead of a self-focused soteriology, such as the Buddhist view that one's own merit brings salvation, the Christian places his or her attention on the atonement provided by Christ on the Cross, though even this grace can be refused. The penalty for bad *karma* in Buddhism is rebirth, but the penalty for a wicked and non-contrite life in Christianity is damnation, or separation from God; the Catholic Church has always affirmed the possibility of eternal and irrevocable damnation, even for Christians. It is often the fear of losing one's salvation that "disposes one to obtain forgiveness in the sacrament of Penance."[58] And the weight of sin is all the more heavy for Christians, who understand that each human person has but one life to attain his salvation.

In addition to the Christian belief that salvation does not derive from attaining good *karma*, but rather from Jesus Christ and one's relationship with him, the Church also teaches that all persons and nations will be judged at a Final Judgment. Saint Matthew's account of this final event is well known to Christians:

> When the Son of Man comes in his glory. All the nations will be gathered before him, and he will separate people one from another as a shepherd separates his sheep from the goats, and he will set

57. *CCC*, 1741.
58. Ibid., 1453.

the sheep on his right hand but the goats at the left. Then the king will say to those on his right hand, "Come, you blessed of my Father, inherit the kingdom prepared for you from the foundation of the world; for I was hungry and you gave me food, I was thirsty and you gave me drink, I was a stranger and you took me in, I was naked and you clothed me, I was sick and you visited me, I was in prison and you came to me." (Matt 25:31–36, 40–43, 45–46)

The *Catechism of the Catholic Church* remarks that, "The Last Judgment will reveal that God's justice triumphs over all the injustices committed by his creatures and that God's love is stronger than death."[59] Belief in such a permanent judgment is rare among Buddhists. In addition to this Final Judgment, Catholic doctrine holds that each individual soul is judged immediately after death in what is called a "Particular Judgment," wherein the soul is transmitted to heaven, purgatory, or hell; but no matter the particular Christian denomination one is attached to, Christianity does not believe in the reincarnation of souls. Salvation is either attained or lost after the course of a single lifetime.

The Buddhist view that after enough lifetimes one may eventually be assured salvation may appeal to even some Christians, though a better knowledge of what Buddhist "salvation" implies, extinction, might seem less appealing in the end than the Christian belief in an eternal freedom from suffering in the presence of God. The pivotal difference between Buddhist and Christian understandings of sin and salvation, as in other areas of difference, lies in the insistent Christian reference to God; sin and salvation can only be accurately understood in light of their relationship to God. When Saint Anselm, the medieval archbishop of Canterbury, turned his attention toward the theological question of salvation, he concluded that Fallen man is incapable of making adequate atonement, but that God's love will not abandon us to our sins. Anselm wrote that, "This debt was so great that, while none but man must solve the debt, none but God was able to do it," and he continues, "so that he who does it must be both God and man."[60] From the Christian perspective, sin is misconduct that rebels against God, and it is God's forgiveness and payment for that sin that principally restores man to God, in whom all salvation ultimately rests.

59. *CCC*, 1040.

60. Anselm, *Basic Writings*, 279.

Q: What is life and death according to Buddhism? What is life and death according to Christianity?

For Buddhists it is more proper to discuss a person's many lives and deaths, and his impermanent soul, while Christianity insists that each person lives and dies only once, but that the soul is eternal. In the *Samyutta-Nikaya Sutra*, the oldest of the Buddhist sutras, a remarkable encounter between the Buddha and a wandering ascetic named Vacchagotta is retold. There were two main schools of thought in India regarding the nature of the soul at that time; the eternalists argued that there is an eternal self, or *atman*, while the annihilationists denied the reality of an eternal *atman*:

> Then Vacchagotta, the wandering ascetic, approached the Blessed One, greeted him courteously, sat down to one side, and said: "Well, now, good Gotama, is there a Self?" The Blessed One remained silent. "Well, then, good Gotama, is there not a self?" Once again, the Blessed One remained silent, and the wandering ascetic Vacchogotta got up and went away.[61]

The Buddha's disciple, Ananda, was puzzled by his silence and asked why he refused to answer whether there is a self or not. The Buddha answered that if he had affirmed or denied either question he would have affirmed or denied the eternalist or annihilationist positions. The final position of the Buddha regarding whether a soul continues or ends, then, is that such concerns "do not tend to edification"; and the Zen tradition would answer there is no "Self" to begin with.

At once the Buddha both denies and accepts the reality of a soul; comfortable with such paradox, however, Buddhism admits the process of birth and rebirth—reincarnation—through which a soul/non-soul finally attains *nirvana*. In plain terms, Buddhism teaches that life and death consist of the undesirable state of *samsara*, or the condition of suffering and illusion caused by being trapped in the cycle of rebirth. All living states are, according to Buddhism, marked by lesser or greater levels of suffering, and thus to escape suffering one must become removed from life and death. To better explain the principal of *samsara*, we must explore the complex Buddhist philosophical understanding of *nirvana*, an idea that has little bearing on Christianity.

---

61. *Samyutta-Nikaya Sutra*, Part 4, 400–401, in Strong, *Experience of Buddhism*, 95–96.

Nagarjuna, one of the foundational thinkers of Buddhist ideas regarding life and death, *samsara* and *nirvana*, wrote extensively on what *samsara* and *nirvana* are in his famous *Mulamadhyamakakarika*, or "Stanzas on the Middle Path." If life is suffering according to the Buddha, and desire is the cause of suffering, then Nagarjuna asks the logical question; as *nirvana*, which is the release from suffering, becomes an object of desire, then is not *nirvana* a secondary cause of suffering? This paradox is perplexing to many Buddhists, not just Christians who have studied Buddhist ideas, and Nagarjuna's answer is to deny that *samsara* and *nirvana* ultimately exist. Consider this mystifying passage from Nagarjuna's Stanzas:

> Freedom [*nirvana*], as a matter of fact, is not existence, for if it were, it would follow that it has the characteristic of decay and death. Indeed, there is no existence without decay and death. If freedom is not existence, will freedom be non-existence? Wherein there is no existence therein non-existence is not evident. If freedom were to be both existence and non-existence, then release would also be existence and non-existence. This too is not proper. The proposition that freedom is neither existence or non-existence could be established if and when existence and non-existence are established.[62]

Nagarjuna seems even to have surpassed the mystery of the Holy Trinity in his ability to describe paradox, for he is stating that *nirvana*, the highest aim of Buddhists, neither exists nor does not exist. Life and death, according to Buddhism, are suffering, and the only release from that suffering is *nirvana*, which is neither a state of existence nor non-existence. Certainly, there are planes of Christian theology that entertain paradoxes, such as considerations of the nature of God, but Christianity need not resort to such inconsistency when it describes the nature of life and death. When answers cannot be logically found in Buddhism, they are often answered with either silence, as the Buddha's reticence in the face of Vacchogotta's questions, or the paradoxical answer/non-answer of Nagarjuna.

In simple terms, the Buddhist understanding of the "purpose and meaning of life" is to escape suffering, which is hopefully accomplished after several lifetimes. Catholicism rejects the theory of reincarnation, for it contradicts what Jesus has taught, and Christians do not view life as merely a state of suffering (*samsara*) from which one should escape. Regarding the

---

62. *Mulamadhyamakakarika*, 25:4, 7, 11, 15. In Fredericks, *Buddhists and Christians*, 61.

Buddhist belief in reincarnation, there are some who argue that the Pythagorean and Brahmanic notion of metempsychosis, the transmigration of a soul into another being after death, is demonstrated by the apparent fact that the souls of some people, as T. Sterling Berry has written, are "able to recollect whence it had come, and why its present condition had been allotted to it."[63] Wordsworth's "Ode on Intimation of Immortality" expresses wonderfully the Christian contrasting view.

> Our birth is but a sleep and a forgetting;
> The soul that rises with us, our life's star,
> Hath elsewhere its setting
> And cometh from afar;
> Not in entire forgetfulness,
> And not in utter nakedness,
> But trailing clouds of glory do we come
> From God who is our home.[64]

If there is any residue of memory with us after birth, as Wordsworth suggests, it is not because we were reborn from another life, but because we have come from God's creative hand. There is no previous life to remember; there is only the one life each person receives from God, to cherish and to take seriously, as there are no other chances to "get it right."

The *Catechism of the Catholic Church*, ever grounded in the Christian commitment to centralize God in all its answers, explains the Christian life in this way: "God, infinitely perfect and blessed in himself, in a plan of sheer goodness freely created man to make him share in his own blessed life," and, "for this reason, at every time and in every place, God draws close to man. He calls man to seek him, to know him, to love him with all his strength."[65] God is the highest form of being and source of happiness, and as we turn our minds and hearts toward him, he in turn "draws close" to us. Søren Kierkegaard has said that, "Our life always expresses the result of our dominant thoughts," and we can attain no better results from our thoughts than when we train our minds on God. In one of his very short, though very emphatic pronouncements, Jesus tells his followers why he has come: "I came so that [you] might have life and have it more abundantly" (John 10:10). Christians do not speak of life as a carrier of suffering, but as

---

63. Berry, *Christianity and Buddhism*, 75.

64. In Van Dyke, *Little Masterpieces of English Poetry*, 91.

65. *CCC*, 1.

a gift from God, who offers his gift beyond this human life, into the next heavenly one.

Q: What does Buddhism teach about the purpose of human existence? What does Christianity teach about the purpose of human existence?

In the previous question, I considered Buddhist and Christian ideas regarding the *nature* of life and death, and here I turn to the *purpose* of life from both perspectives, though it will be clear that these two aspects of human life are interrelated. The difference between how Catholics and Buddhists explain the purpose of human existence is striking. Saint Augustine famously wrote to God in his *Confessions*, "you have made us for yourself, and our hearts are restless until they find peace in you."[66] His cry is echoed in the *Catechism of the Catholic Church*, which states that, "The desire for God is written in the human heart, because man is created by and for God."[67] Buddhism, since it does not believe in a creator God whose creation has a design and reason, views the purpose of human existence as the need to put an end to suffering. One might even argue that Buddhism is centered more on a goal (freedom from suffering) than a purpose (design and reason) of existence, and in fact questions regarding the motive and intention of human life are considered largely irrelevant in Buddhist discourse.

In his discussion of the *Dhammapada Sutra*, or "scripture on the way," Glenn Wallis summarizes the entire message of the Buddha in a single sentence: "The Buddha said repeatedly that he teaches one thing and one thing only: pain and its ending."[68] Considerations of where we came from, and why, are viewed as pointless occupations. Wallis asserts that the Buddha "has no interest whatsoever in giving his listeners (and now readers) answers to questions about creator gods, or about beginnings and ends of the cosmos."[69] The Buddha's response to questions about the origin and purpose of existence can be seen in the *Majjhimanikaya Sutra*, or "middle-length discourses," where he says that such inquiries do "not lead to disenchantment, to dissipation, to cessation, to peace, to direct knowledge, to

---

66. Augustine, *Confessions of St. Augustine*, 17.

67. *CCC*, 27.

68. Wallis, *Dhammapada*, 106.

69. Ibid.

awakening to *nirvana*."[70] In short, the Buddha taught that the major questions asked by other religions, such as Christianity, regarding the source and purpose of human existence are best set aside.

While Buddhism prefers not to ask questions about origin and intention, it does consider how to attain *nirvana*, which is for Buddhists the foremost goal of life, and there are two paths toward enlightenment commonly known as "ordinary" and "extraordinary." The ordinary path to *nirvana* is the method employed by laypersons, and simply includes living properly in order to acquire the merits of good *karma*. For average lay Buddhists, the ordinary path to enlightenment normally takes several rebirths; it is a slower path than the extraordinary one. Hisao Inagaki, a scholar of Pure Land Buddhism, expresses this idea well:

> Ordinary, unenlightened beings repeat cycles of birth-and-death in accordance with the law of karma. One who believes in this law can avail oneself of it to improve his state of existence and finally reach emancipation. The Buddha took great pains to teach his followers and lead them away from painful transmigration.[71]

By living according to Buddhist moral laws and acquiring positive *karma*, the ordinary lay practitioner assures a faster route toward final *nirvana*, but there is another option available to Buddhists, which is the extraordinary path.

The extraordinary path toward enlightenment is the one taken by monks and nuns who have decided to attain *nirvana* in their present life rather than "endure further rebirths." Sometimes called the "Bodhisattva doctrine," the extraordinary path involves a more rigorous commitment to detaching oneself from all desire, and especially the desire for a permanent self. In the *Lotus Sutra*, the Buddha acknowledges how difficult the extraordinary path is, because humans are by nature, "hard to correct, proud, hypocritical, crooked, malignant, ignorant, dull," and "hence they do not hear the good Buddha-call, not once in ten thousand births."[72] In other words, it is difficult to overcome the obstacles of human nature, and thus there are very few who follow the extraordinary path. But in this same *sutra*, the Buddha admits that, "there are others so gifted and so disciplined" that

---

70. See *Majjhimanikaya Sutra* no. 72.

71. Hisao Inagaki, *Three Pure Land Sutras*, 32.

72. Kern, *Lotus*, 65.

they are able to practice his teachings and achieve *nirvana* more quickly.[73] Commonly, it is monks and nuns, living in more conducive circumstances, away from the usual temptations of secular life, who can successfully attain awakening in their current lives. They adopt what Thomas Berry calls the "expedient use of the Nirvana concept."[74]

We can see that Buddhism's understanding of the purpose of human existence is very unlike what is expressed in the Catholic faith; without a belief in a creator God, Saint Augustine's poignant affirmation that we were made for God is not an idea that would likely resonate with Buddhists. The focus of Buddhism, the purpose and goal of all human lives, rather, is the means to eliminate human suffering through following either the ordinary or extraordinary paths toward enlightenment. The ambition of each human, according to Buddhism, is best described as the need to bring an end to all *karmic* results, which in turn sustain human existence, and the existence of all sentient beings, which the Buddha viewed as nothing other than constant anguish.

Other than what is stated in the previous question regarding the nature of human life, which Christians believe is created and oriented toward loving God, what should Christians seek? Perhaps the most obvious answer is in Saint Paul's letter to the Ephesians; the goal of Christians is, he says, "attaining to the whole measure of the fullness of Christ"(Eph 4:13), for it is God's desire that we, as Saint Paul declares in another letter, "be conformed to the likeness of his Son" (Rom 8:29). Christians do not merely wish to be like him in the next life, but to be like him now, in this life. If the goal of a Christian life is to conform oneself to Christ, who is the author of life, it then follows that life is sacred and should be valued. The German theologian and philosopher, Albert Schweitzer, once remarked that, "If a man loses his reverence for any part of life, he will lose his reverence for all of life."[75] It is this created nature of life, and its connection to Christ, that makes life and its purpose meaningful to Christians. To view life as a period of suffering only describes part of the process of living, and even that part brings us closer to Christ. Suffering, for Christians, has value and meaning, and is not always to be "escaped" from. From the Christian view, our attitudes create who we are; Saint Augustine expressed this idea well

73. Ibid., 51.

74. Berry, *Buddhism*, 95.

75. Quoted in Murray, *Prosperity of the Soul*, 156.

when he declared that if we live good lives, the times are also good; as we are, so are the times.

Q: What have Buddhists said about Catholicism?

On the whole, neither Christians nor Buddhists have written much regarding each other's religious traditions during the previous several centuries, but there has been an increase of works in recent decades that compare the two worldviews; perhaps the popularity of Thomas Merton has played a role in the growing interest in associating these two religions. Among Buddhists who have taken an interest in Christian teachings, D. T. Suzuki and Thich Nhat Hanh have been extremely prolific, although the Dalai Lama, whose attention to interreligious dialogue is unprecedented, has also occasionally engaged Christianity from a Buddhist point of view. One of the more unfortunate, and perhaps uninformed, remarks made about Christianity by a Buddhist was made by Suzuki, who suggested that Christianity has had a history of anti-intellectualism:

> . . . intellectual people are generally prone to condemn religion as barring the freedom and obstructing the progress of scientific investigations. It is true that religion went frequently to the other extreme and tried to suppress the just claim of reason; it is true that this was especially the case with Christianity, whose history abounds with regrettable incidents resulting of its violent encroachments upon the domain of reason.[76]

In the same work D. T. Suzuki argues that, "The doctrine of Nirvana is doubtless more intellectual than the Christian gospel of love."[77] It may be granted that at one time or another all religious traditions have collided with scientific and philosophical claims contrary to their belief systems, including both Buddhism and Christianity, but it is arguably the case that Catholic Christianity has historically championed reason as no other faith has as a necessary tool for better understanding creation and truth. And one might equally question Suzuki's contention that the Buddhist notion of *nirvana* is "more intellectual" than the Christian gospel; highly sophisticated thinkers have pointed to inherent contradictions and analytical weaknesses

---

76. Suzuki, *Outlines of Mahayana Buddhism*, 79.
77. Ibid., 58.

within the Buddhist idea of *nirvana*. Other Buddhists, however, have written less pejoratively about Christianity.

The Vietnamese Buddhist monk, Thich Nhat Hanh, has expressed a more positive Buddhist view, though he nonetheless views Jesus as a spiritual master rather than the God and savior he is held to be by Christians. Seeing Christ as both a moral example and an appearance of "God," Hanh notes that, "Love, understanding, courage, and acceptance are expressions of the life of Jesus," and he states that, "God made Himself known to us through Jesus Christ."[78] This Buddhist appreciation of Jesus is well intended, and it marks a positive step toward authentic dialogue, but one must not forget that the Christian understanding of God is very different from what Buddhism believes. For Hanh the Christian doctrine that God and Christ are one and the same is appreciated for its similarity to the Buddhist doctrine of non-duality, which teaches that there are no dualities between any two things, or rather, we might say that according to Buddhism there are no distinctions between anything that exists. In other words, "God," from a Buddhist point of view is sometimes understood to represent the oneness of all things, which suggests that the entire cosmos is in actuality a singular thing, and that a plurality of things is an illusion. To make this point clear, Thich Nhat Hanh asks, "From a Buddhist perspective, who is not the son or daughter of God?"[79] While the Catholic would readily admit that all humans are indeed the sons and daughters of God, they would not assert, as Hanh does, that they are all the children of God in precisely the same way as Christ is.

Catholic intellectuals in recent years have invited Buddhists to engage and comment on Christian traditions, and in the book, *Benedict's Dharma*, Buddhists were asked to read the *Rule of Saint Benedict* and compare Catholic and Buddhist monasticism. Buddhist reactions to Saint Benedict's Catholic rule of spiritual life largely center on the similar monastic practices shared by Catholics and Buddhists, such as robes, prayer beads, and community hierarchy, but disagreements arise over the question of whether there is a God who is distinct from human beings. A Chan, or Zen, Buddhist nun of Taiwan's Foguangshan monastery, Yifa, stated that, "Christian belief in an external source of enlightenment or will is foreign to my own experience in Chan Buddhism," for, as she remarked, it is not Buddhist to surrender to an outside will, for the Buddhist path is completely self-reliant

78. Thich Nhat Hanh, *Living Buddha, Living Christ*, 35.

79. Ibid., 37.

and self-directed.[80] In the end, such intellectual conversations find more agreement on how Catholics and Buddhists can collaborate in charitable services than on similarities of belief, for the Christian belief in an external creator God remains an intellectual obstacle for Buddhist practitioners.

D. T. Suzuki's Buddhist writings have been eclipsed in recent decades by the charismatic presence of the 14th Dalai Lama, whose valuable commitment to promoting compassion and religious tolerance has made a powerful impression on Westerners. In the Dalai Lama's personal memoir, *Freedom in Exile*, he describes his famous encounter with Thomas Merton:

> This was the first time that I had been struck by such a feeling of spirituality in anyone who professed Christianity. Since then, I have come across others with similar qualities, but it was Merton who introduced me to the real meaning of the word "Christian."[81]

This meeting was the 14th Dalai Lama's first exposure to Catholicism with someone who appeared to understand the more nuanced theological claims of Christianity. Among the qualities that the Dalai Lama compliments about Christianity in general include devotion to "calling" and acts of charity, but he does not delve deeply into actual Christian beliefs.

One can locate examples of several Buddhists who have commented privately on Christianity, but since the samgha does not have a formal structure such as the Catholic Church has, there are few "official" Buddhist statements about Christianity. Only scattered remarks appear in various Buddhist writings. Based on scant and disparate Buddhist comments presently available on Christianity, it is clear that further dialogue is necessary, for the doctrinal distance between the two religious traditions remains immense, and still largely misunderstood on both sides. Buddhist platitudes about Christian spirituality and charitable acts do not penetrate the depths of monotheistic theology, and the implications of the Incarnation and Resurrection of Christ remain mostly absent from Buddhist works. And in addition, no matter how appealing it is to declare Jesus and the Buddha "brothers," it gets us nowhere to misrepresent who Jesus himself said he was.

Thich Nhat Hanh's assertion that a Buddhist "*is* the Buddha" may accurately reflect a Buddhist point of view, but when he asserts that "A Christian is a continuation of Jesus Christ: He *is* Jesus Christ, and she *is* Jesus

80. Henry, *Benedict's Dharma*, 80.

81. Dalai Lama, *Freedom in Exile*, 189.

Christ," he is treading on dangerous theological ground without a good deal of explanation.[82] Other questions arise when Buddhists such an Hanh appear to recast Christian concepts in a Buddhist framework; in the section of his book he calls "Touching God, Touching Nirvana," Hanh states that "in nirvana, which is the ground of being equivalent to God, there is no birth, no death, no coming, no going, no being, no non-being."[83] Such easy comparisons, of, say, the God of Christianity to Buddhist *nirvana*, might be tempting for religious syncretists, but they do not accurately represent the Christian understanding of God, who is far from being comparable to "an extinguished flame" (*nirvana*) in Catholic theology. In the end, since Buddhism has no central teaching authority, such as in the Catholic Church, Buddhist statements about Christianity can be infrequent and unsystematic, and quite often misleading.

Q: What has the Catholic Church said about Buddhism?

Unlike Buddhism, the Catholic Church has a hierarchical structure that functions to promote and protect the teachings passed to it by Jesus Christ, and throughout its long history the Church has often needed to respond to the assertions of other religions. One can categorize the Catholic response to Buddhism into two types, official and unofficial. Official statements about Buddhism can be found in such documents as the statements of the Second Vatican Council, the popes, and the *Catechism of the Catholic Church*, which represent the Magisterium, or the teaching authority of the Church; normally the teaching authority of the Church is comprised of the successors of Saint Peter, the pope, and the bishops who assist him. Church teaching (*Ecclesia Docens*), since it is divinely directed, must be observed by all Christians who comprise what is called the Church hearing (*Ecclesia Discens*); the Christian obligation to follow the teaching of the pope and bishops is often called the "assent of faith," and there is nothing in the Buddhist samgha to compare with this Catholic practice. Thus, official Catholic statements on Buddhism tend to be studied and systematic.

Unofficial Catholic statements about Buddhism are far more numerous than official remarks, and unofficial sources consist of such documents as Catholic encyclopedias, Catholic periodicals, books and articles by Catholics, and Catholic media presentations on Buddhism. Unofficial

82. Thich Nhat Hanh, *Jesus and Buddha as Brothers*, 196.
83. Ibid., 10.

statements can be wide-ranging, sometimes contradictory, and an essay on Buddhism from the 1908 *Catholic Encyclopedia*, for example, can be very different from what is said in the *Catholic Encyclopedia* published in our own time. Older documents tend to speak more negatively about Buddhism and use language that would be viewed as uncharitable today. The 1908 *Catholic Encyclopedia* describes Buddhism in this way:

> Another basic defect in primitive Buddhism is its failure to recognize man's dependence on a supreme God. By ignoring God and by making salvation rest solely on personal effort, Buddha substituted for the Brahmin religion a cold and colorless system of philosophy.[84]

In the essay's conclusion, the author, quite derisively asserted that Buddhism was "all but dead," and that European civilization "will inevitably bring about its extinction."[85] Not only are the essay's estimations of Buddhism harsh, but its prediction was entirely incorrect.

Such unconstructive statements do not facilitate entering into dialogue with members of another faith tradition. Scholars today know that Buddhist believers have not so much "ignored" God, as they have not raised the question. In fact, nearly all Eastern religious and philosophical traditions have historically seldom considered the origin of the cosmos or the possible existence of a supreme God; this is not an "Eastern" question. On the other side of the spectrum are the comments on Buddhism made by Thomas Merton and others. Rather than focusing on Buddhism's "defects," Merton chose to highlight Buddhism's more admirable traits, suggesting in his *Mystics and Zen Masters* that Buddhism, "seeks to provide a realistic answer to man's most urgent question: how to cope with suffering."[86] While the 1908 *Catholic Encyclopedia* perhaps too harshly divides Catholic from Buddhist ideals and beliefs, Merton's view of Buddhism tends to at times overly obscure their differences. More official comments on Buddhism published in recent years have been comparatively informed and measured, without compromising or misrepresenting Catholic doctrine.

I have already quoted from the relevant remarks made during the Second Vatican Council, and other comments made by Vatican commissions. Several other Papal remarks are also worth mentioning, in particular because they illustrate the Catholic Church's appeal to Buddhists for

84. Herbermann, *Catholic Encyclopedia*, Vol. 3, 33.

85. Ibid., 34.

86. Merton, *Mystics & Zen Masters*, 286.

collaboration in improving the state of the world. When a group of Japanese Buddhists visited Rome in 1966, Pope Paul VI, welcomed them with warmth, and invited them to, "share in the future contribution of religion to the culture and development of the human family."[87] Yet, the pontiff said these words only after first saying, "We hope that your travels will add to your knowledge of Christianity."[88] When appearing before another group of Buddhists in 1980, John Paul II addressed them with equal esteem, and was sure to remind them that, "On this earth we are all pilgrims to the Absolute and Eternal, who alone can save and satisfy the heart of the human person."[89] Pope Benedict XVI has also commented on Buddhism during his pontificate, acknowledging the shared Christian-Buddhist "respect for life, contemplation, silence, [and] simplicity," and like his predecessors, the Pope turned toward the enduring Christian call to evangelize the world: "In our day too, the Holy Spirit constantly calls convinced and persuasive hearers and preachers of the word of the Lord."[90]

Perhaps one of the most representative remarks the Catholic Church has made regarding Buddhism is included in John Paul II's encyclical, *Redemtoris Missio: On the Permanent Validity of the Church's Missionary Mandate*. In this eloquent apologia for the Church's persistent responsibility to bring the truth of Christianity to the world, the Pope writes:

> I recently wrote to the bishops of Asia: "Although the Church gladly acknowledges whatever is true and holy in the religious traditions of Buddhism, Hinduism, and Islam as a reflection of that truth which enlightens all people, this does not lessen her duty and resolve to proclaim without fail Jesus Christ who is 'the way, and the truth and the life.' . . . The fact that the followers of other religions can receive God's grace and be saved by Christ apart from the ordinary means which he has established does not thereby cancel the call to faith and baptism which God wills for all people."[91]

All of these statements by popes and official Church representatives regarding Buddhism in recent decades reflect the Church's efforts to bridge the cultural spaces that have persisted between religions over the millennia,

87. Paul VI, "Address to Representatives of Japanese Buddhism."
88. Ibid.
89. John Paul II, "Address to Representatives of Buddhism and Shinto in Japan."
90. Benedict XVI, "Post-Synodal Apostolic Exhortation," 122.
91. John Paul II, *Redemtoris Missio*, 55.

and perhaps no other comment exemplifies this ambition more than Pope Paul VI's *Apostolic Exhortation Evangelii Nuntiandi*, wherein he says, "They (non-Christian religions) carry within them the echo of thousands of years of searching for God, a quest which is incomplete but often made with great sincerity and righteousness of heart."[92] The long traditions of spiritual searching in these non-Christian religions, he goes on to say, "are all impregnated with innumerable 'seeds of the Word' and can constitute a true 'preparation for the Gospel.'"[93] What remains to be done, according to Catholic authorities, in addition to creating better cultural awareness and appreciation, is to bring the truth of Christ and his gospel to these religions, which will help that seed grow into the fullness of faith in God.

To reiterate what the Catholic Church has said about Buddhism: it has expressed its admiration for and solidarity with the Buddhist search for understanding and its commitment to human kindness. All those who search, search with eyes that God has made to seek him, but he left his Son and the Church to help searchers turn their gaze toward the fullness of understanding. As Plato has said, "Conversion is not implanting eyes, for they exist already; but giving them a right direction, which they have not."[94]

92. Paul VI, *Apostolic Exhortation Evangelii Nuntiandi*, 53.

93. Ibid., 1.

94. Plato, *Dialogues of Plato*, 352.

SECTION THREE
Scripture, Authority, and Living Buddhism

Q: What is the difference between the Buddhist Sutras and the Bible?

Buddhists do not have a centralized source of doctrinal authority, as do Catholic Christians, nor does Buddhism view tradition as a source of belief. And while Buddhist scripture is not exactly viewed as divinely authored, Buddhists do see their sacred texts as a source for learning the Buddha's teaching, or the Dharma. Buddhism both learns from and venerates the sacred texts of its tradition in a similar way as Christians learn from and venerate the Bible. The Buddhist body of sacred works is commonly known as the *sutras*, a word that implies a "thread" that holds something together or is woven as a textile. The term originally comes from Hinduism, in which the *sutras* normally consist of short aphorisms compiled into a sacred book. Buddhist *sutras* are the canonical scriptures that largely record the life and sayings of the Buddha. In Buddhist terms, the *sutras* are the Buddha's "Dharma body," meaning that once his physical body had disappeared at his final extinction (*parinirvana*), his teachings were preserved in a textual "body" of the Dharma. Just before the Buddha died, he is said to have exclaimed to his disciples, "that which I have proclaimed and made known as the Doctrines and Disciplines, that shall be your Master when I am gone."[1] Following this statement, the Buddha's disciples, like the

1. Quoted in Trainor, *Buddhism*, 176.

86

apostles who followed Jesus, began to recollect their teacher's words and record them as written texts.

Discussing the Buddhist canon, Thomas Berry writes that, "An effort to identify the correct doctrines taught by the Buddha and to fix in permanent form their precise verbal expression was made just after his death."[2] Buddhists generally claim that this project was begun at the First Buddhist Council at Rajagriha in 486 BC. Tradition has it that the Buddha's two senior disciples, Ananda and Upali, each took an important role in the production of the *sutras*; Ananda recited the Buddha's teachings, while Upali recited the rules of discipline for the Samgha. The scriptures that resulted from the First Buddhist Council were two parts of what are known today as the *tripitika*, or "three baskets." From the recitations of Ananda were comprised the *sutra-pitika*, or the "*sutra* basket," which includes thousands of the Buddha's sermons and discourses. Upali's recitations were likewise collected and combined to form the *vinaya-pitika*, or "discipline basket," containing the Buddha's rules for monks and nuns. Around 350 BC, the Third Buddhist Council was convened to clarify doctrines and reject unorthodox beliefs. It was at this Council that the Buddhist *tripitika* canon was completed; the third and final "basket" added to the canon was the *abhidharma-pitika*, or "special teachings basket," which contained commentaries on the other two "baskets." In all, these three groups of texts include the core of Buddhist teaching and the principal scriptures for all Buddhists.

Like the Catholic Church, Buddhism has acquired additional texts that are valued beyond the main *sutras*, but unlike the Catholic Church, Buddhism does not distinguish between "inspired" and "uninspired" scripture. Since the Buddha is not believed to be a god in the Western sense, and since Buddhism has no equivalent of the Christian Holy Spirit, all Buddhist *sutras* are considered sacred and worthy of following, but they are not, as Catholics believe of the Bible, the word of God. Despite this difference, Buddhists revere the *sutras* as holy objects, and as Kevin Trainor points out:

> Like relics, Buddhist scriptures became physical objects to be revered on an altar, buried in the ground to sanctify a site, or placed inside statues of *buddhas* and *bodhisattvas* to transform them from objects of beauty to symbolic representations of the Buddha himself.[3]

2. Berry, *Buddhism*, 69.
3. Trainor, *Buddhism*, 176.

And in addition to the reverence given to the *sutras* as holy objects, believers can also earn merit by recopying and distributing them. In the *Lotus Sutra*, one of Buddhism's most honored *sutras*, the Buddha exhorts: "If anyone, after my extinction, hears this Sutra, and is able either to receive and keep, or himself copy, or cause others to copy it. . . . His merit will be most excellent, infinite and boundless."[4]

Buddhist *sutras* can be compared to Christian scripture in that they are revered as sacred texts that reveal important truths regarding the reality of human existence, but they are not considered to be the inspired word of God. Nor must Buddhism check its scriptures against tradition and authority, as the Bible must be checked in Catholic Christianity. While the Church might respect the human insights contained in Buddhist *sutras*, it recognizes that they do not contain divine revelation, nor do they hold the fullness of truth that is given to humanity by God in the gospels and other inspired texts in the Bible. The Catholic view of the Bible is perhaps best expressed in the opening lines of Henri Daniel-Rops's work, *What is the Bible?*, wherein he writes that in the Bible:

> . . . all there is to say about God and man is said. God's presence pervades it and in it are revealed all those aspects of his mysterious being that we are allowed to glimpse; in it he appears, he speaks and he acts.[5]

In essence, the Bible of the Church is the only holy book wherein man can hear from God himself.

The most esteemed of all *sutras* are those that fit into the Buddhavacana, or "the words of the Buddha" category, and these works are organized differently according to the varying Buddhist sects. In Tibetan Buddhism, for example, the Buddhavacana scriptures are divided into 108 volumes, and include *tantra*, or writings about esoteric rituals and symbols used to attain Buddhahood. Among the more popularly read of the Buddhist *sutras* is the *Dhammapada Sutra*, which is also one of the oldest of the canonical texts. Typical of this *sutra* are short adages such as, "All forms are unreal, he who knows and sees this becomes passive in pain; this is the way that leads to purity," and "Cut down the whole forest of desires, not a tree only."[6] Buddhists believe that the sayings in this *sutra* were recorded on differ-

---

4. Soothill, *Lotus of the Wonderful Way*, 212–213.

5. Daniel-Rops, *What is the Bible?*, 7.

6. Müller, *Wisdom of the Buddha*, 34.

ent occasions when the Buddha spoke in response to various occasions he encountered while with his disciples.

In contrast to Buddhists, Catholics receive the teachings of their faith from three principal sources envisioned like a tripod: authority, tradition, and scripture. Authority to teach the Catholic faith resides in the Church's Magisterium, or teaching authority of the Church, which is passed down through the popes and bishops. Tradition, expressed in the Latin *tradere* ("to give down"), is the transmission of doctrines, information, or practices, from one generation to the next. In a nutshell, tradition is "the handing down from mouth to mouth of truths which have been revealed by God but which are not manifested in Holy Scripture."[7] Thus, the Council of Trent pronounced that:

> All truth and discipline are contained written in the books and the non-Written Traditions, which being received by the Apostles from the mouth of Christ himself, or under the inspiration of the Holy Ghost, being delivered to us, as it were, by hand, came to us.[8]

Distinct from tradition, which is passed down outside of written texts, the Christian Bible is the actual word of God written down under the inspiration of the Holy Spirit.

The *Catechism of the Catholic Church* provides perhaps the most concise Christian definition of the nature of the Bible: "God is the author of Sacred Scripture. 'The divinely revealed realities, which are contained and presented in the text of Sacred Scripture, have been written down under the inspiration of the Holy Spirit.'"[9] The *Catechism* goes on to explain how Scripture must be interpreted in light of Tradition:

> As a result, the Church, to whom the transmission and interpretation of Revelation is entrusted, "does not derive her certainty about all revealed truths from the holy Scriptures alone. Both Scripture and Tradition must be accepted and honored with equal sentiments of devotion and reverence."[10]

In a poignant portrayal of the Christian understanding of divine revelation in the Bible, *Dei Verbum*, one of the principle documents of the Second

7. *New Catholic Encyclopedia*, 969.

8. Council of Trent, "Ep. Fund," C. V.

9. *CCC*, 105.

10. Ibid., 82.

Vatican Council, states that, "In His goodness and wisdom God chose to reveal Himself and to make known to us the hidden purpose of His will. . . ." and, "Through this revelation, therefore, the invisible God out of the abundance of His love speaks to men as friends and lives among them."[11] Pope Leo XIII said this in another way long before the Council in his encyclical on the study of Holy Scripture when he noted that in the Bible, God makes known to man, "by supernatural means, the hidden mysteries of His Divinity, His wisdom and His mercy."[12]

The Bible, then, is nothing less than God speaking to man, and the Catholic view of Scripture is perhaps best summarized in the words of Saint Jerome, who said that, "Ignorance of the Scriptures is ignorance of Christ."[13] Not only does the Bible contain the actual Word of God, unlike the Buddhist understanding of the *sutras*, but it is besides a profound form of prayer; the Bible is, as Saint Augustine says, a "hymn to Christ":

> The Scriptures are in fact, in any passage you care to choose, singing of Christ, provided we have ears that are capable of picking out the tune. The Lord opened the minds of the Apostles so that they understood the Scriptures. That he will open our minds too is our prayer.[14]

Q: Who is the leader of the Buddhist Samgha? Who is the leader of the Catholic Church?

Many are tempted to look for parallels between Catholicism and Buddhism, especially since they appear to share visible similarities. Catholics have patriarchs; Buddhists have patriarchs. Catholics have an ordained clergy; Buddhists have an ordained clergy. Catholics have monastic communities with monks and nuns; Buddhists have monastic communities with monks and nuns. Catholics have a rich liturgical tradition; Buddhists have a rich liturgical tradition. But despite these external parallels, the Catholic Church and the Buddhist Samgha are more different than similar, and one of the major differences lies in the notion of leadership in the two communities. Within the Buddhist Samgha there is no central leader,

11. *Dei Verbum*, 2.
12. Leo XIII, *Providentissimus Deus*, 1.
13. Quoted in *CCC*, 133.
14. Quoted in Jeffrey, *Luke*, 287.

which might surprise some Westerners who have become accustomed to seeing the Dalai Lama as the "pope" of Buddhism. It should be remembered that until 1959, when the current Dalai Lama fled Tibet into India, few people outside of Asia had ever heard of a "Dalai Lama," and the majority of practicing Buddhists only tangentially paid attention to the Tibetan sect of Buddhism. Since then, however, his popularity has grown to such a level that for all intents and purposes, the Dalai Lama seems to be the leader of all Buddhists; in reality he is the leader of only one sect, the Yellow Hat sect, of Tibetan Buddhism.

There are too many hierarchies in Buddhism to recount them all here in this short book, and there are similarly too many different schools of Buddhism, each with its own understanding of leadership, to provide an account of each branch within the Samgha. It will suffice to say that while there is not a single "leader" in Buddhism, as there is in Catholicism, there are many leadership roles in the community, such as patriarchs, important reincarnations, and secular rulers who support and direct the Buddhist Samgha. Several schools claim to have a patriarch who oversees its members, and one of the best examples is the patriarch of the Zen, or Chan, school. The main concern for Buddhists regarding leadership is the diffusion of the Dharma and the role that leaders play in its correct and effective transmission. In Zen, it is the patriarch who ensures orthodoxy, and in fact, Zen claims that its, and only its, lineage of Buddhist teaching represents the correct Dharma taught by the Buddha himself. According to Zen teaching, the first transmission of the Dharma occurred on Vulture Peak, or Griddhraj Parvat in India, where the Buddha was given a flower and asked to give a sermon on the Dharma.

This story recalls that the Buddha, rather than directly speaking aloud, held out the flower in front of his disciples, and only Mahakasyapa responded; when he saw the flower, Mahakasyapa simply smiled. His smile is believed by Zen Buddhists to represent the fact that only he fully understood the true Dharma. And seeing his reaction, the Buddha reportedly said, "I am the owner of the eye of the wonderful Dharma, which is Nirvana, the mind, the mystery of reality and non-reality, and the gate of transcendental truth," after which he exclaimed, "I now hand it [the eye] over to Mahakasyapa."[15] Zen followers declare that their first patriarch was Mahakasyapa, and thus only the Zen line of patriarchs has protected the Buddha's true teachings. As Holmes Welch puts it, "The Chinese eventually

15. Quoted in Suzuki, 12.

worked out a genealogy tracing the transmission, generation by generation, from Mahakasyapa to Bodhidharma," who was the first Zen patriarch to teach the "authentic Dharma" in China.[16] It is not unexpected that several branches of Buddhism claim that their own patriarchs are the only bearers of the Buddha's accurate Dharma. The hierarchical system adopted by Tibetan Buddhism, based on the reincarnation of important persons, is less exclusive in terms of its claim to the "true Dharma," but the Tibetan system does largely monopolize the reincarnations of powerful Buddhist teachers.

What makes the Dalai Lama the recognized leader of Tibetan Buddhism is the fact that Tibetan Buddhists believe him to be the reincarnation of one of Buddhism's most admired bodhisattvas, known as Avalokiteshvara, or Guanyin in China. Avalokiteshvara is popularly venerated as the bodhisattva of compassion, and is often represented as a man, or woman, encircled by thousands of arms reaching out to help those who call out to him. This is why the Dalai Lama has made compassion one of the central marks of his public speaking. The belief that certain bodhisattvas or powerful lamas can be reborn into human beings is called the *tulku* system, and it is held that such masters can choose the circumstance and location of their next incarnation.

When a powerful lama, which means a "chief" or "high cleric" in Tibetan Budddhism, dies, such as the Dalai Lama, Tibetan Buddhists eagerly anticipate the reappearance of the lama's next life, and once he is found he is customarily reinstalled into his previous position of leadership. One of the major questions that non-Tibetan Buddhists have regarding the *tulku* system is whether a powerful lama can be reborn as a non-Tibetan. The Tibetan Buddhist scholar, Jamgon Taye, has indicated that, "Although some children born to parents outside the Himalayan region have been recognized as reincarnate masters, these represent but a tiny fraction."[17] Among the thousand or so *tulku* reincarnations, perhaps less than a dozen such reincarnations are non-Tibetan. While the Dalai Lama is the most powerful lama in the Tibetan *tulku* system, this does not mean that he or any lama is considered by other Buddhist schools to be higher ranking than any other Buddhist leader.

Another important area of leadership within the Buddhist community is a position known as a *dharmaraja*, or "righteous king." In principle, a righteous king is a secular ruler, or king, who is himself a devout Buddhist

16. Welch, *Practice of Chinese Buddhism*, 156–57.

17. Taye, *Enthronement*, 26.

and endeavors to support and protect the Buddhist Samgha in his domain. In our own time, the king of Thailand is the most famous *dharmaraja*, since he is the acknowledged leader of the Buddhist community in his country, which is one of the few officially Buddhist nations.

The first *dharmaraja* is acknowledged to have been King Ashoka, discussed previously. Being filled with remorse for massacring the people of Kalinga, Ashoka, "began to study the teachings of various sects, visited monks frequently, learned from them, and formally dedicated himself as an adherent of the Samgha."[18] Once he had converted to Buddhism, King Ashoka applied the Dharma to the management of his empire and established Buddhist pilgrimage sites throughout his realm, distributing important relics to around 84,000 stupas, or mound reliquaries. In addition to making Buddhism the official religion of his empire and establishing thousands of pilgrimage locations, Ashoka installed stone monuments inscribed with Buddhist edicts. In one such edict, Ashoka outlined the administration of his empire:

> My officials of all ranks—high, low, and intermediate—act in accordance with the precepts of my instruction. For these are the rules: to govern according to the *dharma*, to administer justice according to the *dharma*, to advance the people's happiness according to the *dharma*, and to protect them according to the *dharma*.[19]

All subsequent righteous kings have followed the precedents of King Ashoka, and in turn the Samgha in Buddhist countries such as Cambodia and Thailand have, for the most part, obeyed the instructions of their *dharmaraja* rulers.

As we can see, it would be inaccurate to discuss any single person as "the leader" of the Buddhist community; rather, there are several different types of Buddhist leaders, such as patriarchs, important reincarnated persons, and righteous kings. The Catholic Church, on the other hand, recognizes a single leader who is divinely appointed by God to lead all baptized Christians. Among the teachings of the Catholic Church, the principle of Church unity under one leader is among the most important, and the Church claims that it is the only visible institution founded by Jesus Christ. Full unity with Christ's Church is attained only by being in communion with the pope, who is the successor of Jesus' chief apostle, Saint Peter.

18. Robinson, *Buddhist Religions*, 58.
19. Quoted in Trainor, *Buddhism*, 50–51.

Catholic Christians rely on scriptural and historical evidence to make this assertion. Biblical confirmation of Peter's primacy and leadership of the Church begins with John 1:42; when Christ first met Peter he said, "You are Simon, the son of John; you shall be called Cephas." Christ spoke to him in Aramaic, and called Peter "Cephas" (or "Kepha"), meaning "stone" or "rock." Such a name was never used at that time, and thus Jesus had a special role in mind for Peter. The Catholic understanding of Peter's leadership of all Christians is discerned in several passages in Scripture: Peter received the first converts into the Church (Acts 2:41); Peter imposed the first ecclesiastical punishment (Acts 5:1); Peter performed the first miracle (Acts 3:1); Peter made the first official ecclesiastical visit (Acts 9:32); and so forth. Thus, the Catholic Church continues to obey what it perceives to be God's desire that Peter and his successor bishops of Rome lead the Christian faithful as their supreme pontiff.

The Catholic belief in Christian unity is a significant distinction from Buddhism; whereas Buddhists, even with their visible community, place emphasis on the individual's quest for *nirvana*, Catholic Christianity places emphasis on the collective and shared nature of Christian worship and the journey toward salvation. Pope Boniface III was an eloquent apologist for Christian unity under a single leader. In his papal bull, *Unam Sanctam*, Boniface wrote that the Church is:

> ... that seamless garment of the Lord which was not cut but which fell by lot. Therefore of this one and only Church there is one body and one head—not two heads as if it were a monster: Christ, namely, and the vicar of Christ, Saint Peter, "Feed my sheep." My sheep, He said, using a general term, and not designating these or those particular sheep; from which it is plain that He committed to him all His sheep.[20]

The visible unity of the Christian Church under the pope, Catholics argue, responds to Jesus' affirmation that, "there shall be one flock, one shepherd" (John 10:16), for, as Christians, we deeply honor the humility and proper order that comes from deference to leadership, especially leadership that was appointed by God. And finally, the Catholic Church, even during times of internal and external failure, believes itself to remain the visible body of Christ and the visible sign of God's kingdom on earth. Saint John Chrystostom judiciously reminded the Christians of his era that the Christian community will always remain a testament to Christ's love for mankind: "It

---

20. Boniface III, *Unam Sanctam*.

is an easier thing for the sun to be quenched," he said, "than for the Church to be made invisible."[21] Buddhism has no visible or structural equivalent to the Catholic understanding of the papacy and the Church.

Q: What is the basis of Buddhist morality? What is the basis of Christian morality?

Buddhist moral teachings are centered on the acquisition of good *karma*, or positive merit, and fundamentally, these teachings focus first on one's own advancement rather than the advancement of others. The others-first approach of Christianity is, in a certain sense, foreign to Buddhist moral teaching, which might at first appear curious in light of Buddhism's active promotion of compassion and acts of charity. The essential nature of the doctrine of *karma* is self-focused, for as the Buddha told his disciples just before he died, "work out your salvation on your own with diligence." This does not mean, however, that Buddhists do not care about the welfare of others and the results of human moral actions. Buddhists do indeed care about the wellbeing of others, though their motivation for, and method of, good moral behavior is approached from a distinctively Buddhist point of view. A common Zen aphorism states that, "What one does is what happens to him." This may sound similar to Jesus' famous exhortation from the gospel of Saint Matthew: "So whatever you wish that men would do to you, do so to them" (Matt 7:12). Buddhists, however, often suggest that the Christian code of behavior is centered on moral commandments, whereas Buddhist ideas of good actions center on principles. Buddhist moral principles tend to be more flexible than Christian commandments. This makes sense in light of Buddhism's very different understanding of truth.

One of the key traits of Buddhist moral teaching is that there is no ultimate truth to dictate personal behavior; moral decisions are made based more upon an inner disposition that is influenced by the teachings of the Buddha and an understanding of the laws of *kharma*. University of San Diego Buddhist nun and professor of religion, Karma Lekshe Tsomo, explains Buddhist moral teaching in this way:

> There are no moral absolutes in Buddhism and it is recognized
> that ethical decision-making involves a complex nexus of causes
> and conditions. "Buddhism" encompasses a wide spectrum of

---

21. Quoted Rhodes, *Visible Unity of the Catholic Church*, vol. 1:24.

beliefs and practices, and the canonical scriptures leave room for a range of interpretations. All of these are grounded in a theory of intentionality, and individuals are encouraged to analyze issues carefully for themselves. . . . When making moral choices, individuals are advised to examine their motivation—whether aversion, attachment, ignorance, wisdom, or compassion—and to weigh the consequences of their actions in light of the Buddha's teachings.[22]

The principle assertion in this quote is that Buddhism claims no "moral absolutes." Buddhist moral teaching, since it is not concerned with the design and desire of a creator God, tends to emphasize personal intention rather than performance, for Buddhism does not believe that an external force, or God, will judge one's performance after she or he dies; only *karma* propels one's destiny during life and after death.

Buddhist scholar, Harvey Aronson, contrasts the Buddhist preference for intention to the Western notion of performance by comparing Buddhist moral expectations to the statement of Saint Paul in Romans, where we see the passage, "I do not understand my own actions. For I do not what I want, but I do the very thing I hate" (Rom 7:15). For a Catholic Christian, human nature is inclined toward sinfulness as a result of the Fall, so Saint Paul acknowledges that humans default toward poor behavior; we must rely on God's Word and the Holy Spirit to help us choose the correct path. According to Aronson's Buddhist worldview, however, Saint Paul's remarks represent a "tragic vision concerning the individual's capacity to rationally move themselves [sic] forward," calling the Christian view a form of "self-doubt."[23] Aronson suggests that Westerners are at least in part attracted to Buddhism because of its emphasis on "self-help" in moral decision-making.

Few can deny that Buddhists, like Christians, have performed profoundly good humanitarian acts, and Buddhist promotion of compassion as a necessary virtue for human goodness is commendable, but the foundation of Buddhist humanitarianism and compassion is the belief that good acts to others are performed for their value to one's own *karmic* future. In one of Buddhism's most revered *sutras*, the *Udana*, the Buddha outlines this principle:

My thought has wandered in all directions throughout the world. I have never met with anything that was dearer to anyone than his own self. Since to others, to each one for himself, the self is

22. Tsomo, "Prolife, Prochoice: Buddhism and Reproductive Ethics."

23. Aronson, "Buddhist Practice," 67.

dear, therefore let him who desires his own advantage not harm another.[24]

The Buddha's exhortation cleverly turns the human tendency for selfishness into a principle for good behavior, for by being good to others one earns *karma* dividends, so to speak, which will pay off in the future. Another aspect of the Buddha's teaching here is the notion that those around us are not really distinctly different beings; the Buddhist idea of the ultimate oneness of all things means that to mistreat others is largely to mistreat oneself. Catholic Christianity promotes the same tenets of humanitarianism and compassion, as can be seen in the Catholic Church's position as the world's largest humanitarian institution; but God, rather than the self, is the central reason and model for Catholic morality.

In more concrete terms, Buddhist morality is expressed in certain formulas that are to be followed less as rules than as principles, and other than the Five Buddhist Precepts, the most common formulas for moral action are outlined in three of the Eightfold Paths. The third path, "Right Speech," includes "refraining from lying, from slander, from harsh speech, and from frivolous speech"; the fourth path, "Right Action," emphasizes "refraining from taking life, from taking what was not given, and from sexual misconduct"; and the fifth path, "Right Livelihood," suggests "refraining from any forms of livelihood that would compromise fulfillment of other aspects of the eightfold path."[25] Taken by themselves these moral ideals fit nicely with Catholic teaching, but the Buddhist belief in reciprocity as the reason for good actions is unlike the Christian understanding of the effects of the Fall, God's role in human redemption, and the reality of God's laws revealed in Scripture. And in addition, Buddhist principles of moral conduct tend to be variable according to varying senses of what constitutes good and bad *karma*.

The Buddhist notion that moral tenets are not based upon an absolute truth contrasts starkly with the Catholic view of truth. Shortly before he was named Pope Benedict XVI in April 2005, Cardinal Joseph Ratzinger warned that humanity is "moving toward a dictatorship of relativism which does not recognize anything as definitive and has as its highest value one's own ego and one's own desires."[26] Without the notion that truth, which is unchangeable, dictates moral behavior, persons are left to modify moral

24. Quoted in Maurice Percheron, *Buddha and Buddhism*, 95.
25. Wallis, *Dhammapada*, 156.
26. Ratzinger, Pre-Conclave Homily.

laws based on "new understandings" or "pluralistic" standards. In other words, when what Jesus and the Church teach are disregarded in favor of prevailing desires or trends, humanity or individual persons can adjust "moral regulations" to discard Christian values. The axiom, "as long as it doesn't hurt anyone else it's perfectly fine," can justify a multitude of behaviors forbidden in Christianity. *Karma* is often defined in this way; moral laws can be changed, "as long as no one else is hurt." This is an incorrect view according to Christianity, for there exists a God whose laws remain immutable; Christians trust that God knows better than humans what is right and what is wrong.

Catholic morality is understood to come from God's Word in Scripture, which sets out to recognize the human dignity of all persons. In a word, Catholic morality is about life, for it was Jesus who said, "I came that they may have life, and have it abundantly" (John 10:10). In its discussion of Catholic moral teaching, the *Catechism of the Catholic Church* includes an astute quotation from Saint Leo the Great:

> Christian, recognize your dignity and, now that you share in God's own nature, do not return to your former base condition by sinning. Remember who is your head and of whose body you are a member. Never forget that you have been rescued from the power of darkness and brought into the light of the Kingdom of God.[27]

Morality, then, is deeply connected to the fact that we were created in the image of God, have individual souls, and are called to honor and protect the purity of our own dignity and the dignity of others. And to know what we must and must not do to remain pure and safeguard this dignity, God speaks through Scripture and the teaching authority of the Church.

Throughout the gospels, Jesus calls persons to love others, to place others before oneself, and before even these, to "Love the Lord your God with all your heart and with all your soul and with all your strength and with all your mind," and to, "Love your neighbor as yourself" (Luke 10:27). The Christian understanding, unlike the Buddhist one, affirms that morality can only be properly ordered when God is the centerpiece of one's love and obedience. God's laws are not subject to the whims and nuances of modern "reinterpretations." As David Bohr describes Christian morality:

> This then, in sum, is the good news, the Christian story line: God creates; we sin. God redeems us through a new creation in Christ.

27. Leo the Great, *Sermo 21 in nat. Dom.*, 3: PL 54, 192C. Cited in *CCC*, 1691.

We now are expected to live our lives according to the Christ we have received.[28]

Moral laws were created and ordained by God; they must be lived by man. The results of our moral behavior does not affect *karma*; it is judged by God. To fully understand and live a moral life one must live "life in Christ," for as Saint Paul says, "Whoever is in Christ is a new creation" (2 Cor 5:17).

Q: What are the Buddhist teachings on human sexuality? What are the Church's teachings on human sexuality?

Few issues in contemporary society have been more divisive than human sexual morality; homosexuality and sex outside of marriage have become more culturally mainstream. From the Buddhist point of view, sexual morality is a highly contested question, for the principal concern of the Buddha was less focused on what specific actions are acceptable or forbidden, than on the role sexual desire has on *kharma* in general. In one *sutra*, the Buddha states, "that one can engage in sensual pleasures without sensual desires, without perceptions of sensual desire, without thoughts of sensual desire—that is impossible."[29] The Buddha's concern here is not with the details of what is sexually proper, but with the effects of desire, which is, according the Four Noble Truths, the root cause of suffering. One could interpret the Buddha's comment here to suggest that all sexual activity is discouraged in Buddhism, as it involves desire, which propels *karma*, and thus suffering. Buddhist *sutras* do, however, contain occasional references to sexual activities outside of marriage, though we must acknowledge that even Buddhist marriage is viewed differently than Christian marriage.

In the *Saleyyaka Sutra*, or "Brahmans of Sala Scripture," the Buddha prohibits sexual intercourse with a married or betrothed person as a form of "unrighteous conduct."[30] In fact, this form of misconduct is mentioned in the same category as killing. In one Buddhist account, Ananda receives negative *karma* after intercourse with a married woman:

28. Bohr, *Catholic Moral Tradition*, 25.

29. Bhikkhu Bodhi, Alagaddupama Sutta, in *The Middle Length Discourses of the Buddha*, 227.

30. Bhikkhu Bodhi, Saleyyaka Sutta, in *The Middle Length Discourses of the Buddha*, 380.

> When Ananda was born as a blacksmith he sinned with the wife of another man. As a result he suffered in hell for a long time and was born for fourteen existences as someone's wife, . . . and it was seven existences more before his evil deed was exhausted.[31]

The question of homosexuality in Buddhism is much more complex. On the one hand, Buddhist leaders have disparaged same-sex relationships, while the practice of homosexuality has also been an active part of Chinese, Japanese, and other Asian cultures.

The famous sixteenth and seventeenth-century Catholic missionary to China, Matteo Ricci, remarked with distress how common homosexuality was in Buddhist China:

> That which most shows the misery of these people is that no less than the natural lusts, they practice unnatural ones that reverse the order of things, and this is neither forbidden by law nor thought to be illicit nor even a cause for shame. It is spoken of in public and practiced everywhere without there being anyone to prevent it.[32]

While there can be little doubt of the historical prominence of homosexual relationships among Chinese and Japanese Buddhist practitioners, Buddhist leaders, such as the current Dalai Lama, have spoken against same-sex associations.

Before meeting homosexual Buddhist leaders in 1997, the Dalai Lama offered some remarks on his position regarding same-sex relationships. The Dalai Lama stated:

> We have to make a distinction between believers and unbelievers. . . . From a Buddhist point of view, men-to-men and women-to-women is generally considered sexual misconduct. From society's viewpoint, mutually agreeable homosexual relations can be of mutual benefit, enjoyable and harmless.[33]

While he suggests that homosexuality is "misconduct," he also implies that this rule may only apply to Buddhists. In general, Tibetan Buddhism's stance on sexual morality is very similar to Catholicism; both have traditionally prohibited sex outside of marriage, homosexual intercourse, and masturbation.

---

31. Malalasekera, 1960: 267–268. Quoted in Peter A. Jackson, "Male Homosexuality and Transgenderism in the Thai Buddhist Tradition," http://www.enabling.org.

32. Quoted in Dynes and Donaldson, *Asian Homosexuality*, vii.

33. Quoted in Lattin, "Dalai Lama Speaks on Gay Sex."

Without a belief in a creator God, revealed Scripture, or a single visible moral leader, such as the pope of Rome, Buddhism's moral teachings on sexual issues are left to interpretation. Buddhism does not find it necessary to carefully define specifically moral and immoral acts. The main concern for Buddhists, as I have said, is not for whether an action such as homosexuality is or is not moral, but rather with the problem of sexual desire in general. As José Cabezón has stated: "Buddhist texts take a consistently negative stance toward all expressions of sexuality as being impediments to spiritual progress."[34] Thus, it can safely be argued that one of the major differences between Buddhist and Catholic teaching about human sexuality is that while Buddhism views sexuality as a cause of desire that prevents one from attaining *nirvana*, traditional Catholic teaching accepts human sexuality as God created, healthy, and encouraged, given that it is enjoyed within the limits of God's intention. Regarding human sexuality, Buddhists are more likely to argue how sexual behavior affects human suffering than to argue whether a certain type of sexual practice is "natural" or "unnatural," "acceptable" or "sinful."

Catholic teaching on issues of sexual morality has remained, many Catholics would argue, unchanged for two millennia, though some Christians have in recent years re-evaluated or reinterpreted the Church's moral teachings about human sexuality. In the 1930s, all mainline Protestant denominations condemned such behaviors as artificial contraception, divorce, abortion, euthanasia, adultery, the viewing of pornography, and homosexual behavior. Presently, the Catholic Church, the Orthodox, and only a few Protestant communities remain largely consistent with their past and still hold these practices to be "disordered," and they preserve their beliefs based on an enduring interpretation of the teachings of Christ. Rather than rely solely on human reason, the Catholic Church seems to rely principally on the Word of God for its understanding of human sexuality.

The Ten Commandments, for example, address questions of sexual morality; one condemns adultery (Exod 20:14, 17) and another forbids coveting a neighbor's wife (Deut 5:18, 21). In the gospel of Saint Matthew, Jesus is seen reinforcing these commandments: "You have heard that it was said, 'You shall not commit adultery.' But I say to you that every one who looks at a woman lustfully has already committed adultery with her in his heart"(Matt 5:27). And regarding the foundation and purpose of marriage and sexuality, Jesus refers to the Creation account in Genesis:

34. Cabezon, *Buddhism, Sexuality, and Gender*, 210.

> Have you not read that he who made them from the beginning
> made them male and female, and said, 'For this reason a man shall
> leave his father and mother and be joined to his wife, and the two
> shall become one flesh?' So they are no longer two but one flesh.
> What therefore God has joined together, let no man put asunder.
> (Matt 19:4)

The traditional Catholic interpretation of this passage is that Jesus places the sacredness and purpose of human sexuality within the realm of marriage between a man and a woman, and binds all sexuality to that realm.

In addition to Scripture, Catholic Christianity teaches that human reason, informed by Natural Law, can recognize the proper order of human sexuality. The great theologian, Thomas Aquinas, is one of the most powerful voices of human reason enlightened by Natural Law, and he wrote that:

> the rational creature is subject to Divine providence in the most
> excellent way, in so far as it partakes of a share of providence, by
> being provident both for itself and for others. Wherefore it has a
> share of the Eternal Reason, whereby it has a natural inclination to
> its proper act and end: and this participation of the eternal law in
> the rational creature is called the natural law.[35]

In other words, as Charlie Price has summarized what Saint Thomas says here, it is irrational to put molasses instead of oil into the engine of a car.[36] One must act according to the nature of things if they are to function correctly. That God has given humanity his divine guide to right and wrong, and that this guide is supported by Natural Law, is conceptually foreign to Buddhist moral theory. In contrast to the theory of *karma*, which can be imprecise when discussing specific sexual acts, Christianity relies upon the Word of God and the voice of human reason instructed by Natural Law to understand what is morally acceptable and unacceptable in the area of human sexuality. Indeed, even within Catholic Christianity the interpretation and implementation of Natural Law is presently being debated, but the preference for life remains an unquestioned value in Catholic moral teaching on human sexuality. The Church affirms all human sexual acts that are rightly oriented toward life, and in his encyclical, *Casti Connubii*, Pope Pius XI rather strenuously wrote that an immoral sexual act, "is deliberately frustrated in its natural power to generate life," and "is an offense against

---

35. Aquinas, *Summa Theologicae*, I–II Q91 a2, corp.

36. Price, *50 Questions on the Natural Law*.

the law of God and of nature."[37] God himself created man from his divine desire to produce life out of nothing. It is clear then that the Buddhist criticism of all desire, even what Catholic Christianity has traditionally viewed to be the properly ordered desire for sexual acts, is contrary to the Christian understanding of the purpose and moral limits of human sexuality.

Pope John Paul II tirelessly reminded all people that sexual morality is bound to the family and to the desire of the family to promote life. In his message for the twenty-seventh World Day of Peace in 1984, the Pope said:

> The family, as the fundamental and essential educating community, is the privileged means for transmitting the religious and cultural values which help the person to acquire his or her own identity. Founded on love and open to the gift of life, the family contains in itself the very future of society; its most special task is to contribute effectively to a future of peace.[38]

Q: Is abortion allowed in Buddhism? Is abortion allowed in Catholic Christianity?

Since Buddhism has no central teaching authority and no clear scriptural instructions by the Buddha regarding the morality of abortion, Buddhist statements about abortion are diverse, and opinions vary. The first law of the Buddhist Five precepts instructs all Buddhists to abstain from killing, and many Buddhists suggest that this pertains to abortion, as it is viewed as a form of killing. Just as in Christian and secular circles, the question of when human life begins is hotly debated among Buddhists, though the earliest Buddhist monastic code expressed that life begins at conception. Only in recent decades, as secular governments have begun to legalize abortion, has Buddhism begun to reinterpret the early Buddhist restriction against the killing of children still in the womb.[39] As Peter Harvey describes the traditional Buddhist view, one can "no more 'excuse' abortion than the killing of an adult who might be reborn as a human."[40] But Buddhist discourse on the acceptability of abortion has grown more complex, and as Harvey states, "A crucial issue, though, is *how* evil is it and what 'other things' can

---

37. Pius XI, *Casti Connubii*, 56.
38. John Paul II, "Message for the XXVII World Day of Peace."
39. See Harvey, *Introduction to Buddhist Ethic*, 311–320.
40. Ibid., 315.

come to outweigh this evil, so that abortion comes to be seen as a 'necessary evil' in certain circumstances."[41] Without a central authority the realm of conditions in Buddhist teaching where the "necessary evil" of abortion has become justifiable has grown more expansive.

In an interview with the *New York Times*, the Dalai Lama refered to abortion as "an act of killing and is negative," but he clarified his opinion to confess that there are exceptions to this negative. "I think abortion should be approved or disapproved," he said, "according to each circumstance."[42] He went on to say that, "If the unborn child will be retarded or if the birth will create serious problems for the parent, these are cases where there can be an exception."[43] Such statements as these by the Dalai Lama have aroused some Buddhists to criticize him, because previous monastic rules demanded that monks who help or support women to have an abortion must be expelled from the Buddhist community. Even so, in some regions, such as Japan, abortion has been increasingly tolerated by Buddhist followers. After an induced abortion or miscarriage, Japanese women have traditionally participated in a Buddhist-Shinto ceremony called the *mizuko kuyo*, or "fetus memorial rite." In Taiwan, women still practice a ritual called *yingling gongyang*, meaning "fetus ghost memorial service," during which women appease the ghosts of aborted fetuses to assuage their sense of guilt after having an abortion.[44]

Buddhists in Europe and the United States have interpreted the morality of abortion according to circumstance; Western Buddhists tend to be even more Relativistic regarding the moral acceptability of abortion than their counterparts in the East. The American Tibetan Buddhist lama, Jeffrey Miller, who now goes by the name Surya Das, provides a common view of abortion among US Buddhists in his popular book, *Awakening the Buddha Within*:

> The question of motivation is always relevant in Buddhism. Why was the decision to have an abortion made? Was it made carelessly and without much consideration, or were there substantial reasons, perhaps? Was the health and safety of the mother either physically or emotionally a realistic issue?[45]

41. Ibid., 351.

42. Dalai Lama, "The Dalai Lama," interview.

43. Ibid.

44. Moskowitz, *The Haunting Fetus*.

45. Surya Das, *Awakening the Buddha Within*, 216.

One sees the Buddhist doctrine of *karma* clearly below the surface of Lama Surya Das's remarks, but there is also a more modern perspective, one that more freely justifies abortion when there are "substantial reasons."

The American Tibetan Buddhist nun and professor in the Religious Studies department at the Catholic institution, the University of San Diego, Karma Lekshe Tsomo, reveals her preference for the rhetoric of "prochoice," which is so prevalent in US society:

> In the end, most Buddhists recognize the incongruity that exists between ethical theory and actual practice and, while they do not condone the taking of life, do advocate understanding and compassion toward all living beings, a lovingkindness that is nonjudgmental and respects the right and freedom of human beings to make their own choices.[46]

Karma Lekshe Tsomo speaks here principally on behalf of the mother's choice, rather than on behalf of the aborted child, suggesting that Buddhist "lovingkindness" is "nonjudgmental" and respects a woman's (but, many Buddhists suggest, not the child's) freedom to make her own choice. In the same discussion, she quotes another Buddhist, Lama Thubten Yeshe, who asserted that, "If you know, beyond a shadow of a doubt, that you are creating happiness rather than suffering for a being by killing it, then go ahead."[47] To be fair, the lama qualifies this statement by suggesting that only "a person with a very high level of spiritual realization can be completely sure" about whether she (or he) is actually "creating happiness rather than suffering" for the future life of the child.

While Buddhism, especially in the Western context, tends to disparage "moral absolutes," Catholic Christianity adopts a different view. Relying on the Bible as God's Word to mankind, the Church has formulated its response to abortion based on its understanding of the divine will and order of the creator. Psalm 139 includes a keen description of the unborn child:

> For you created my inmost being, you knit me together in my mother's womb. I praise you because I am fearfully and wonderfully made; your works are wonderful, I know that full well. My frame was not hidden from you when I was made in the secret place. When I was woven together in the depths of the earth, your eyes saw my unformed body. (Ps 139:13–16)

46. Karma Lekshe Tsomo, "Prolife, Prochoice."

47. Ibid.

Catholicism argues that from conception, God is at work in the womb, and to interrupt God's work and intention is largely unimaginable to Catholic Christian thinking. In Saint Luke's gospel, we read that Jesus and John the Baptist, who were both still in their mothers' wombs, "greet" one another: "It happened, when Elizabeth heard Mary's greeting, the baby leaped in her womb, and Elizabeth was filled with the Holy Spirit" (Luke 1:39–45). In other words, the unborn are human persons, with the same value and dignity as those already born.

Early Christian non-canonical texts also proscribed the practice of abortion, and we find in the *Didache*, or "Teaching of the Twelve Apostles," a work that dates to the end of the first century AD, the statement: "Do not kill a fetus or commit infanticide."[48] The *Catechism of the Catholic Church* is equally unambiguous regarding the Catholic view of abortion. In its discussion of "respect for human life," the *Catechism* affirms that:

> Human life must be respected and protected absolutely from the moment of conception. From the first moment of his existence, a human being must be recognized as having the rights of a person—among which is the inviolable right of every innocent being to life.[49]

The Church speaks plainly; the rights of an unborn child are not less important than the rights of the mother, or any other person for that matter, and the child is described as an "innocent being," unable to speak on his or her own behalf. And referring to early Christian texts such as the *Didache*, the *Catechism* continues to assert that, "Since the first century the Church has affirmed the moral evil of every procured abortion," and continues to note that, "Direct abortion, that is to say, abortion willed either as an end or a means, is gravely contrary to the moral law."[50]

Conscious of what it perceives as the irrational and self-interested impulse behind moral relativism, the Catholic Church has confirmed that not only individual persons, but also governments, are subject to God's instruction against abortion. In an official statement, the "Instruction on Respect for Human Life in its Origin and the Dignity of Procreation," the Church states that every level of society is morally bound to respect human life at all stages:

48. Jefford, *The Didache in Context*, 356.

49. *CCC*, 2270.

50. Ibid., 2271.

> The inalienable rights of the person must be recognized and re-
> spected by civil society and the political authority. These human
> rights depend neither on single individuals nor on parents; nor
> do they represent a concession made by society and the state; they
> belong to human nature and are inherent in the person by virtue
> of the creative act from which the person took his origin. Among
> such fundamental rights one should mention in this regard every
> human being's right to life and physical integrity from the moment
> of conception until death.[51]

In the conclusion of this important document, the Church affirms the
words of Jesus Christ, who said to his followers, "What you do to one of the
least of my brethren, you do unto me" (Matt 25:40).

Perhaps one of the most summoning voices of the Catholic Christian
view of abortion was the founder of the Missionaries of Charity, Mother Teresa of Calcutta, who cared for the "least of her brethren," and who argued
that, "Abortion is the greatest threat to peace." She declared this during a
1985 television interview with Thom O'Connor, and in another section of
their discussion she reminds us that the unborn baby is created, "in the image of God for greater things, to love and be loved," which is "why it is such
a terrible thing to think that the mother, to whom the child has been given
as a gift of God, could destroy it."[52] In equally emphatic terms, Mother Teresa addressed abortion at the National Prayer Breakfast in Washington,
D.C, in 1994:

> But I feel that the greatest destroyer of peace today is abortion,
> because it is a war against the child—a direct killing of the inno-
> cent child—murder by the mother herself. And if we accept that a
> mother can kill her own child, how can we tell other people not to
> kill one another?[53]

Speaking directly about the situation America, she continued, saying that,
"Any country that accepts abortion is not teaching the people to love, but
to use any violence to get what they want."[54] Mother Teresa represents, perhaps, one of the most vocal Catholic apologists for the Church's pro-life
position.

51. Congregation for the Doctrine of Faith, "Instruction on Respect for Human Life
in its Origin and the Dignity of Procreation," III.

52. Mother Teresa, Thom O'Connor Interview with Mother Teresa.

53. Mother Teresa, National Prayer Breakfast in Washington, D.C.

54. Ibid.

In contrast to the pervasive Buddhist view of abortion today, especially in Western countries, that it can be acceptable in certain conditions and is a "matter of choice," the Catholic view is comparatively resolved; all humans share the same dignity as God's creation from the instant of conception, and it is morally wrong to kill a child under any condition. In his *Evangelium Vitae*, or "The Gospel of Life," John Paul II wrote at length about the Christian position against abortion, and in what is perhaps his strongest statement, he said that, "Among all the crimes which can be committed against life, procured abortion has characteristics making it particularly serious and deplorable," and he reasserted the Second Vatican Council's statement that abortion is, "together with infanticide, an 'unspeakable crime.'"[55]

Q: What does Buddhism teach regarding human dignity and social justice? What does Catholicism teach regarding human dignity and social Justice?

Among the areas of similarity and difference between Buddhists and Christians, the urgent call to improve the world's social justice problems is perhaps a vocation in which both traditions may best collaborate. The foundational principle of Buddhist social teaching is the notion of *karuna*, which is often appropriately translated as "compassion." Some Buddhists, such as Theravada Buddhists, understand the practice of (or "dwelling in") *karuna* as a means of attaining a happy present life or an improved rebirth due to one's exceptional acquisition of personal merit (*karma*). For Mahayana Buddhists, on the other hand, *karuna* is among the requisites for becoming a bodhisattva. For the Theravada Buddhist, *karuna* is often refered to as one of the four "divine abodes," along with loving kindness, sympathetic joy, and equanimity. These "abodes" are imagined much like directions of a compass, and thus we see it mentioned in the *sutras* in this way:

> He keeps pervading the first direction—as well as the second direction, the third, and the fourth—with an awareness imbued with compassion. Thus he keeps pervading above, below, & all around, everywhere & in every respect the all-encompassing cosmos with an awareness imbued with compassion: abundant, expansive, immeasurable, free from hostility, free from ill will.[56]

55. John Paul II, *Evangelium Vitae*, 58.

56. *Kalama Sutta*, quoted Thanissaro Bikkhu (Geoffrey Degraff) *Handful of Leaves:*

This passage from the *Kalama Sutta*, and passages in other similar *sutras*, express *karuna* as an effort to remove harm and suffering from others, and is based on an understanding of the sameness and connectedness of all things. As one Buddhist text on the idea of *karuna* advises, "Strive at first to meditate upon the sameness of yourself and others. In joy and sorrow all are equal; thus be guardian of all, as of yourself."[57]

Perhaps the best-known manifestation of Buddhist compassion today, as it is related to the work of social justice, is the recent emergence of a movement known as "engaged Buddhism," sometimes called, "socially engaged Buddhism." Followers of this form of Buddhist social action trace the movement's origin to the Vietnamese teacher, Thich Nhat Hanh, who was a friend of Thomas Merton. The general approach of engaged Buddhists is to apply such tenets as *karuna* and various meditation practices to improve conditions of environmental, political, and social suffering and injustice. Related efforts to promote social justice today are found in the "humanistic Buddhism" movement, which teaches that compassion begins from an awareness of the interconnectedness of the self and others, and centers on the understanding that actions toward others are also actions toward the self. Such declarations evade the Buddhist conundrum of discussing "self" and "other" in light of the Buddha's strong negation of such concepts, but terms such as "engaged" Buddhism and "humanistic" Buddhism represent an attempt to redirect the historical Buddhist tendency to retreat from society, toward a compassionate engagement with society to help solve its serious social problems.

Humanistic Buddhism emphasizes the central "oneness" of all persons and things, and draws from this idea to formulate pragmatic ways in which Buddhists can improve the world. In his book, *Humanistic Buddhism: A Blueprint for Life*, Hsing Yun describes humanistic Buddhism in this way:

> Humanistic Buddhism stresses the purification of life through ethical thought, and the elevation of both mind and spirit. If you believe in the Law of Cause and Effect and practice it in your life, then the Law of Cause and Effect is Humanistic Buddhism. If you believe in compassion and practice it in your life, then compassion is Humanistic Buddhism.[58]

Volume Three, 33.

57. Shantideva, *Way of the Bodhisattva*, 122–23.
58. Hsing Yun, *Humanistic Buddhism*, xviii–xix.

Such ideals are not too distant from Catholic ideas at first glance, but when he later describes the Buddhist impulse toward social justice as helping others to attain "peace in this life" by "embracing everything with its nature of emptiness," the two religions appear somewhat distinct.[59]

Many Buddhist organizations have emerged in recent years to promote charitable acts and social justice, such as the Buddhist Peace Fellowship, based in Berkeley, California, the International Network of Engaged Buddhists, established in Thailand, and the Zen Peacemakers, founded in Yonkers, New York. One recent expression of the emergent Buddhist charity and social action movement is Buddhist Socialism, which has been largely influenced by the writings of the Southeast Asian Buddhist philosopher, Buddhadasa Bhikkhu, who has suggested that in "advanced" religious spirituality there is no such thing as religion.[60] Buddhadasa Bhikku and his fellow Buddhist Socialists argue in favor of a politicized and Socialist form of Buddhism that employs what they call "Dharmist Socialism" to eliminate social classes. This Socialist turn has attracted positive attention as well as criticism from other Buddhists; criticisms focus especially the Buddhist Socialist use of Buddhism more as a convenience than a religious belief system.

What perhaps distinguishes Buddhist from Catholic Christian ideals of social justice even more than its philosophical and political disparities is the difference between how Buddhists and Christians define the human person and human dignity. When discussing the Buddhist notion of the human person, Buddhism scholar, Mikio Matsuoka, asserts that, "Buddhism is a human-centered religion," and notes that the Buddha, "taught that the fundamental cause of suffering in the world must not be sought in the external environment, but within the human heart." "Opposite of being escapist," Matsuoka continues, "this approach naturally leads to tangible social reform."[61] In other words, the Buddha taught that human persons must seek relief from suffering only within their own "human heart," and that "social reform" results from one putting her or his own heart, or mind, in order. While this is not entirely off the path of Christian thinking—certainly Christians must attend to their own thoughts and behaviors—the Buddhist view, being a "human-centered religion" that is inwardly-focused, overlooks, as Christianity holds, that human dignity is attained principally

59. Ibid., xix.
60. See Buddhadasa Bhikkhu, *Handbook for Mankind*, especially pages 5–8.
61. Mikio Matsuoka, "Buddhist Concept of the Human Beingi," 51.

in that persons are created in God's image, and that they are imbued with an eternal soul. Human dignity and social reform cannot be properly fulfilled, according to Christian teaching, without God's involvement.

The Buddhist and Christian understanding of human dignity and social justice may be summarized in this way: whereas Buddhism understands human dignity and compassion to be "endowed in the lives of all human beings" without the presence of "and external higher power," Christianity believes that both derive mainly from the fountain of God's divine love.[62] Matsuoka expresses the Buddhist concept in this way: "When discussing the Buddhist view of human dignity, the Mahayana Buddhist concept that all living beings alike possess the Buddha nature is often cited."[63] The Buddha nature described here is the nature that is "already enlightened," the nature that has "already escaped from suffering." Human dignity from this view, then, is based not on our value as beings created in the divine image of God, but as beings that already share in the Buddha's understanding of the causes of suffering and the impermanence of the human "self."

The Catholic view of the human person and social justice, which is perhaps more appropriately referred to as the Catholic "social teaching," is as one can imagine, rooted deeply in the teachings of Christ in Scripture. The Church's understanding of human dignity and its social teaching are interrelated ideas. Very simply put, Christianity believes that each human person has inherent value and distinction because she or he was created in the likeness of God.[64] What this means is that human value, regardless of cultural identity, race, sex, or economic status, is viewed as a reflection of God the creator. Human dignity is not based upon one's spiritual understanding or state, but is rather an immutable divine gift from God.

When Cardinal Timothy Dolan addressed an audience at the University of Notre Dame in 2011, he asserted that the Church understands each person's dignity to flow from the fact that he is, "a child of God, his creation, modeled in his own image, destined for eternity," and this vision of the sacredness of the human person, "gave rise to the greatest system of health care, education and charity the world has ever known."[65] The Catholic Church has been and remains an active and widespread charitable

62. Ibid., 56.

63. Ibid., 57.

64. See Genesis 1:26–27.

65. Dolan, "Archbishop Dolan Defines Human Dignity as 'Primary Doctrine' of Church."

institution, and it is so precisely because of its belief in God and human dignity in relation to God. The *Catechism of the Catholic Church* affirms also that, "the dignity of the human person is rooted in his creation in the image and likeness of God," and adds to this, that "with the help of grace they grow in virtue, avoid sin, and . . . attain to the perfection of charity."[66] One notices here again the sustained Christian belief that human worth, human self-improvement, and human charity are inseparable from each person's likeness to God and God's constant attention to human suffering and needs.

Catholic social teachings, informed by its understanding of human dignity, centers on the Christian call to perform acts of charity and engage matters of economics, social organization, and to help alleviate the suffering caused by poverty. According to Pope Benedict XVI, the goal of Catholic social teaching is furthermore connected to human reason:

> simply to help purify reason and to contribute, here and now, to the acknowledgment and attainment of what is just. . . . [The Church] has to play her part through rational argument and she has to reawaken the spiritual energy without which justice. . .cannot prevail and prosper.[67]

Charity begins, as the Pope states, in conjunction with reason; it is not merely the expression of an emotional impulse, for emotion un-tempered by reason rarely outlasts a passing mood.

One way to envision Catholic social teaching is to imagine how a holy icon is viewed in the Eastern Church. When one looks at an icon, one actually sees who is depicted, whether it is God, the Blessed Virgin, angels, or the saints. Since all humans are a likeness of God, all humans are, in a real sense, icons; by seeing a human one also perceives God, the creator. Once one begins to see other human persons as reflections of, or windows to, God, then it stands to reason that the dignity of every person must be valued and safeguarded. Based upon these principles, John XXIII, wrote his famous encyclical, *Pacem in Terris*, or "Peace on Earth," during the Cold War, plagued as it was with the constant threat of international conflict. He wrote:

> Once again we exhort our people to take an active part in public life, and to contribute towards the attainment of the common good

66. *CCC*, 1700.

67. Benedict XVI, *Deus Caritas Est*, 28.

of the entire human family as well as to that of their own country. They should endeavor, therefore, in the light of the Faith and with the strength of love, to ensure that the various institutions—whether economic, social, cultural or political in purpose—should be such as not to create obstacles, but rather to facilitate or render less arduous people's perfecting of themselves both in the natural order as well as in the supernatural.[68]

Based on its religious commitment to the teachings of Jesus Christ and Scripture, the Church has not failed to engage all areas of society, from the most powerless to the most empowered.

In his 1987 work, *Sollicitudo Rei Socialis,* or "On Social Concern," Pope John Paul II called for the urgent engagement of Catholics in matters of social justice, and he insisted that charity "is not a feeling of vague compassion or shallow distress at the misfortunes of so many people, both near and far." "On the contrary," he said, "it is a firm and persevering determination to commit oneself to the common good; that is to say, to the good of all and of each individual, because we are all really responsible for all."[69] He also maintained that genuine compassion and a determination for the common good is based on the Christian understanding of God's design and part in the workings of men and women. In a word, Buddhism purports to serve charitably as a "human-centered" act, while Catholicism purports to serve charitably as a "God-centered" act.

Q: What are prayer and meditation from the Buddhist and Catholic perspectives?

Before discussing prayer and meditation as they relate to Catholic Christianity and Buddhism, it is important to reaffirm the importance of clear and precise language, for as Plato asked, "In good speaking, should not the mind of the speaker know the truth of the matter about which he is to speak?"[70] What Plato suggests in his question is that, since reality is made intelligible through words, our words must accurately represent the reality about which is spoken. Words make little sense if we cannot agree on what they mean. The modern philosopher, Josef Pieper, in his book, *Abuse of Language, Abuse of Power,* argues that authentic communication stops, and

68. John XXIII, *Pacem in Terris,* 146.
69. John Paul II, *Sollicitudo Rei Socialis,* 38.
70. Plato, *The Works of Plato,* 303.

propaganda begins, when words are incorrectly used to influence people rather than truthfully represent reality.[71] I mention the importance of the accurate and truthful use of language because of recent claims by some Christians that Buddhists "pray," or that Buddhist meditation is an "alternative form of prayer." Such assertions misrepresent the differences between Christian prayer and Buddhist meditation; the term "Buddhist prayer" is as misleading as the term "Zen Catholicism."

To begin with a brief definition of Buddhist meditation: If the reader has read the previous descriptions of *nirvana*, then it will be readily clear that since the goal of Buddhist meditation techniques is the attainment of *nirvana*, it is, some would argue, difficult to justify such techniques for Christian use. The traditional word to describe Buddhist meditation is *bhavana*, which derives from the root *bhu*, a word that implies "becoming," or the independent process of arousing a particular mental state. *Bhavana* is any practice employed to better facilitate the attainment of *nirvana*, and what most Westerners imagine when they discuss Buddhist meditation is a specific form of *bhavana* known as *dyana*, or "sitting meditation."[72] In fact, the Chinese word Chan and Japanese word Zen, both derive from *dyana*. When one pictures the tranquil Zen practitioner sitting cross-legged in what appears to be a deep state of mental consideration, one is envisioning the traditional Buddhist practice of *dyana* meditation, which is a form of *bhavana* cultivation.

In his book, *Stages of Meditation*, the Dalai Lama explains at length that Buddhist meditation techniques are designed to inculcate one's mind with the teachings (*dharma*) of the Buddha, to free the mind of its own deluded sense of self. This is how he describes *dyana*:

> The whole purpose of meditation is to lessen the deluded afflictions of our mind and eventually eradicate them from their very roots. By learning and practicing the profound and vast aspects of the [Buddha's] teaching, a practitioner with prolonged familiarity with and meditation on selflessness eventually gains understanding of reality.[73]

Just as Christian prayer is designed to facilitate Christian objectives, Buddhist meditation is designed to facilitate the Buddhist objective to attain what the Dalai Lama calls "Dharma Knowledge," that is, to enter into a

71. See Pieper, *Abuse of Language, Abuse of Power*.

72. See Gregory, *Traditions of Meditation*, especially p. 19.

73. Dalai Lama, *Stages of Meditation*, 21.

mental state wherein one's thoughts grow aware of one's non-existence, or selflessness.

There are several schools of Buddhism, each one differing slightly in how it approaches the practice of meditation, though by and large most Buddhists agree that the goals of meditation include "mindfulness," "tranquility," "supramundane powers," and certain "insights" important to attaining *nirvana*. Despite the common Western misconception that Buddhist mindfulness simply implies "full awareness" of one's present moment, Buddhists understand it in a more technical way. Mindfulness, or *sati*, suggests a spiritual ability to view things "correctly." In other words, Buddhist mindfulness means seeing all things in light of the Buddha's teachings on reality. Tranquility, or *samatha*, from a Buddhist point of view, is a mental state that is unmoved by any desire, good or bad (though, good and bad largely is a rejected dichotomy in Buddhism). One way to help achieve this mental state is to create a calm environment, within which one is comparatively free from distractions. But again, Buddhist tranquility is sought only to assist one's movement toward *nirvana*.

Supramundane powers, or *Iddhi*, imply a mental state brought about by Buddhist meditation techniques that Buddhists believe allows one to know the mind of others. But other supernatural powers Buddhists have traditionally considered possible through meditation include flying, vanishing and reappearing, passing through solid objects, and traveling to other worlds. Tibetan Buddhism is the most active school that believes in and seeks such powers, and there are common legends among Tibetan Buddhists of powerful lamas who are believed to have vanished while meditating, sometimes leaving their hair and fingernails behind as a sign of their former presence. The insights, or *vipassana*, sought through Buddhist meditation are expected to provide an enlightened understanding of the "true nature" of reality. Simply said, *vipassana* means that one has at last gained insight into the Buddha's "three marks of existence." These include *anicca*, or the notion that all things are impermanent; *dukkha*, the realization that the sustained existence of a "self" results only in suffering; and *anatta*, the Buddhist belief that there is no "self" to begin with. Carl Bielefeldt, who has devoted considerable time to studying the meaning and practice of Zen meditation techniques taught by the famous Zen master, Dogen, summarized sitting meditation, called *zazen* in Japanese, in this way:

Indeed (at least when rightly practiced) *zazen* was itself enlightenment and liberation; it was the ultimate cognition, the state he
called "nonthinking" (*hi shiryo*) that revealed the final reality of
things; it was the mystical apotheosis, the "sloughing off of body
and mind" (*shinjin datsuraku*), as he said, that released man into
this reality.[74]

There is little in such practice that can be reconciled with the aim of Christian prayer; Christianity would find little benefit in *zazen*, which is directed
toward "nonthinking" and the erasure of "body and mind."

To reiterate, Buddhist meditation consists of certain techniques designed to enable mental states conducive to *nirvana*, or liberation from
"self"; Christian prayer is oriented in an entirely different direction. Buddhist meditation induces an inwardly focused mental state that better
equips one to understand, as the Dalai Lama describes it, "Dharma knowledge." Prayer, on the other hand, encourages God-focused worship, communication, and reflection, wherein one grows more aware of God's divine
will and presence. The Christian concept of prayer comes from the Latin,
precari, which means "to plead" or "to ask earnestly." To pray, as a Christian
understands prayer, means that there is someone there to whom one makes
her or his request. Throughout the Bible one is told both how to pray, and
to do so often. Jesus recommended:

Ask and it will be given to you; seek and you will find; knock and
the door will be opened to you. For everyone who asks receives;
the one who seeks finds; and to the one who knocks, the door will
be opened. (Matt 7:7–8)

And St. Paul wrote simply, "Pray continually" (1 Thess 5:17).

Meditation is one form of Christian prayer, but Buddhist meditation,
since its goal is *nirvana*, is not a form of Christian prayer. It can be argued
that Buddhist meditation is designed to direct one's thoughts *away* from
God, for a belief in a God would be an "obstacle" to *nirvana*. For Jesus,
on the other hand, prayer and meditation turn a person resolutely toward
God, and we have no better example of how a Christian should pray, what
she or he should say, and to whom her or his prayer should be directed,
than the prayer taught by Jesus himself:

This, then, is how you should pray: "Our Father in heaven, hallowed be your name, your kingdom come, your will be done, on

74. Bielefeldt, *Dogen's Manuals of Zen Meditation*, 3.

earth as it is in heaven. Give us today our daily bread. And forgive us our debts, as we also have forgiven our debtors. And lead us not into temptation, but deliver us from the evil one." For if you forgive other people when they sin against you, your heavenly Father will also forgive you. But if you do not forgive others their sins, your Father will not forgive your sins. (Matt 6:9–15)

Jesus' example of how to pray is petitionary and, above all, directed purposefully toward God. There is nothing here that alludes to an induced "mental state" or attaining a condition of "nonthinking."

It would be incorrect, however, to suggest that there is no such thing as mystical prayer in Christianity, though Christian mysticism, unlike Buddhist mysticism, is immersed in the name and reality of God, or Jesus Christ. The Jesus Prayer of the Eastern Church is one example: "Lord Jesus Christ, Son of God, have mercy on me a sinner." This invocation, typically said repeatedly, can integrate one into what Eastern Christianity calls a form of mental *ascesis*, or asceticism that clears away worldly distractions and allows one to more intimately communicate with God. The *Catechism of the Catholic Church* states that:

> The name of Jesus is at the heart of Christian prayer. All liturgical prayers conclude with the words "through our Lord Jesus Christ." The Hail Mary reaches its high point in the words "blessed is the fruit of thy womb, Jesus." The Eastern prayer of the heart, the Jesus Prayer, says: "Lord Jesus Christ, Son of God, have mercy on me, a sinner." Many Christians, such as St. Joan of Arc, have died with the one word "Jesus" on their lips.[75]

Jesus Christ, as the *Catechism* says, is the center and reference point of all Christian prayer and meditation; non-Christian meditation practices, such as Buddhist sitting (*zazen*), are arguably directed in entirely different directions because they seek mental emptiness, emptiness even from—or perhaps especially from—the notion of and belief in God.

Centering Prayer

Since the 1970s many Catholic churches and retreat centers have offered classes and sessions on what is called "centering prayer," a spiritual practice developed by the Trappist monk, Father Thomas Keating, based largely on

75. *CCC*, 435.

Buddhist and Hindu meditation techniques. While he served as the abbot of St. Joseph's Abbey in Spencer, Massachusetts, Keating hosted discussions with Buddhist and Hindu practitioners, and invited a Zen meditation master to explain Buddhist meditation to the monks at the monastery. In his book, *Intimacy with God*, Keating asked:

> Could we put the Christian tradition into a form that would be accessible to people . . . who have been instructed in an Eastern technique and might be inspired to return to their Christian roots if they knew there was something similar in the Christian tradition?[76]

Abbot Keating invited a former Trappist monk who had become a Transcendental Meditation instructor to teach this form of "mantra meditation" at the abbey. Transcendental Meditation, rooted in Hinduism, involves repetitive recitation of a sound, or a "transformative" syllable *mantra*, which is practiced for 15 to 20 minutes twice per day in order to erase distracting thoughts.

Centering "prayer" boasts an ability to help one find the center of her or his being, and there find the God within. For those who have formally studied Buddhist and Hindu forms of meditation, it is abundantly clear how the ideas expressed in these non-Christian religions have influenced and permeated Keating's novel form of "prayer." In his introduction to Cynthia Bourgeault's book, *Centering Prayer and Inner Awakening*, Keating attempts to distinguish his own method of centering prayer from Buddhist meditation by suggesting that while Buddhism practices "mindfulness," his practice may be understood as "heartfulness." Ironically, in East Asian languages, the heart and mind is the same thing, and in Keating's new centering prayer, heartfulness and Buddhist mindfulness also appear to be the quite the same thing.[77]

According to his critics, the most disconcerting aspect about Keating's creative mixing of Christian prayer and Buddhist-Hindu meditation is that he has combined Christianity with religious practices that deny the difference between God and man. Christian prayer seeks a relational encounter with God; God and man are not the same. One does not seek to find the "God within" in Christian prayer, but rather to commune—communicate—with

76. Keating, *Intimacy with God* 15. Also see Dreher, "The Danger of Centering Prayer," 14–16.

77. Keating, "Forward," in Cynthia Bourgeault, *Centering Prayer and Inner Awakening*, especially pp. 6–7.

God (creator), who is wholly other from man (creation). In a lengthy discussion of Keating's centering practices and their possible incompatibility with Christian prayer, Father John Dreher refers to centering prayer as a "form of self-hypnosis," which makes use of *mantras* to invoke a particular mental state that, Keating believes, enables one to capture the indwelling God within. In contrast to this practice, Dreher outlines a more commonly held understanding of Christian prayer:

> The fact that God indwells us does not mean that we can capture him by techniques. Nor does it mean that we are identical with him in our deepest self. Rather, God indwells us by grace which does not blend human and divine natures. On the contrary, it perfects and empowers our limited human faculties, so that we can relate to him. We can no more manipulate this indwelling of grace by psychological techniques than we can manipulate our existence.[78]

Responding to the growing popularity among Christians to combine Eastern spiritual techniques with Christianity in the 1970s, the Orthodox priest, Archimandrite Sophrony, has expressed how some Christians have responded to the practice of centering prayer:

> Such exercises have enabled many to rise to suprarational contemplation of being, to experience a certain mystical trepidation, to know the state of silence of mind, when mind goes beyond the boundaries of time and space. In such like states man may feel the peacefulness of being withdrawn from the continually changing phenomena of the visible world, may even have a certain experience of eternity. But the God of Truth, the Living God, is not in all this.[79]

Liturgy, Mysticism, and Lectio Divina

If Buddhist meditation cannot replace Christian prayer, and as many argue, should not be combined with Christian prayer, one might ask what methods of prayer already exist within the Christian tradition that one may turn to instead. Catholic tradition has richly inherited a multitude of options, as one can expect after two thousand years of history. In general, the Catholic Church acknowledges several types of prayer to God: mental prayer, vocal

78. Dreher, "The Danger of Centering Prayer."
79. Archimandrite Sophrony, *His Life is Mine*, 116.

prayer, postures of prayer, and meditative prayer. Certainly, the Jesus Prayer is promoted as spiritually beneficial to Christians of both the Eastern and Western Churches, and many Catholics point out that the Mass or the Divine Liturgy are the highest and most beneficial forms of prayer available to Christians. Catholics often underscore that in the Eucharist one can commune with God by receiving the real Body, Blood, Soul, and Divinity of our Lord and Savior, Jesus Christ, in Holy Communion. The Catholic Church also recognizes a form of prayer, or Christian meditation, that is experienced by some, known as a "mystical union," when one is fully occupied with the Divine; one might refer to this experience as an "ecstasy," such as was experienced by Saint Teresa of Avila. Such a mystical union is not attained by techniques; it is a gift from God who bestows this gift of his own initiative.

The Benedictine practice of *Lectio Divina*, or "divine reading," has become increasingly popular in recent years among Catholics; it is a powerful method of accessing God through his Word. At a meeting with over 400 Scripture experts in 2005 during a congress in Rome on "Sacred Scripture in the Life of the Church," Pope Benedict XVI remarked that "if this practice is promoted with efficacy, I am convinced that it will produce a new spiritual springtime in the Church."[80] How better can one commune with God, many Christians ask, than to read and contemplate God's Word? Traditionally ascribed to Saint Benedict and Pope Gregory I, divine reading normally consists of seven stages: *statio* (position), *lectio* (reading), *meditatio* (meditation), *oratio* (prayer), *contemplatio* (contemplation), *collatio* (discussion), and *actio* (action). In the initial stage, *statio*, one is encouraged to find a comfortable and quiet place, which may include holy images, candles, or incense.

One begins by breathing slowly while focusing on the Holy Name of Jesus, and nothing else, and once the reader is suitably tranquil, she or he traces the sign of the Cross on the Scripture, kisses the place where the Cross was made, and begins to read the Word with unhurried and gentle attention. After the passage has been read, the reader then meditates on the text—visualizing it, contemplating its divine mysteries, and pondering its symbolism and shadows. What is the Holy Spirit saying through the text? There is no need for supplementation; neither *mantras* nor *zazen* sitting can add to the Word of God or help gain insight into its meaning. Saint Benedict understood the practice of meditating on sacred Scripture

---

80. "Pope Benedict XVI Promotes Biblical Meditation."

in *Lectio Divina* to be essential to the spiritual maturity of a monk, and stipulated the specific times and manner of this practice in his Rule. Saint John Chrysostom artfully described the importance of this form of Christian prayer and meditation when he said, "To get the full flavor of an herb, it must be pressed between the fingers, so it is the same with the Scriptures; the more familiar they become, the more they reveal their hidden treasures and yield their indescribable riches."

CONCLUSION

Truth and Dialogue

There is an ancient Chinese notion that "dialogue is the making of friends." As important as friendship is, this is not the only Western understanding of dialogue. Dialogue is also the collaborative quest for truth, and as long as truth is avoided for the sake of harmony there cannot be authentic dialogue, for only in truth can genuine peace be found. There can be little doubt that one of the manifest strengths of Matteo Ricci's missionary enterprise in China was his tireless effort to befriend the Chinese people, and in his famous treatise, *De amicitia*, or "On Friendship," he wrote: "If we know the value of friends, every time we go out to meet people, we will not return home without seeking to make a new friend."[1] Even a cursory reading of Ricci's private journals reveals that while friendships were important to Ricci, nothing was more important to him as a missionary than gaining souls for Jesus Christ. Li Tiangang's statement that, "In the past one hundred years or so, few foreign missionaries have realized that it was more important to 'make friends' in China than to 'preach the Gospel,'" betrays a misunderstanding of why Christian missionaries leave their home countries, for they believe that nothing is more important than preaching the gospel.[2] According to Matteo Ricci, his greatest successes were not his friendships, but his conversions, for in his view, what better gift could he have given his friends in China than friendship with God?

If at times statements have seemed "polemical" in this book it is not because I wish to create antagonism, or even to diminish what is good and noble in Buddhism, but I have rather sought respectful clarity, for truthfulness is the only enduring basis for progress, and friendship for that matter.

1. Quoted in Torrens and Xiaoxin Wu, *Edward Malatesta*, 88.
2. Li Tiangang, "Father Malatesta and the Chinese Scholars," 88.

And here I wish to add an appeal to people of all religious traditions to recognize our shared commitment to human kindness, charity, and collaboration, for argumentation and conflict will get us nowhere, as we have seen in two World Wars and September 11, 2001. In the middle of the last century, the Indian philosopher Radhakrishnan had already begun to write about the growing globalization of our planet. "For the first time in the history of our planet, its inhabitants have become one whole, each and every part of which is affected by the fortunes of every other," he wrote, and continued to lament:

> And yet the sense that mankind must become a community is still a casual whim, a vague aspiration, not generally accepted as a conscious ideal or an urgent practical necessity moving us to feel the dignity of a common citizenship and the call of a common duty.[3]

In other words, Ricci's plea for friendship, beyond religious difference, has not yet been entirely heard, for the old and stubborn attachments to nationalism, cultural dominance, colonial power, and submission remain deeply embedded in the human spirit. If we seek truth, and if we seek it together, we shall become better friends in the process, and most importantly, perhaps we will find what we search for.

In her book with the provocative title, *A New Religious America: How a "Christian Country" Has Become the World's Most Religiously Diverse Nation*, Diana Eck shows convincingly how America, after the Immigration and Naturalization Act of 1965, has come to host a more diverse religious mix than any other place on earth.[4] "Contact," James Fredericks rightly suggests, "is not community," and we live in an era that calls for community more than ever.[5] Some convincingly argue that it is secular nation states, not religious groups, that have caused most of the world's recent tension and violence, and this is precisely why religious groups must become peaceful collaborators, a living example of community, that can stand against secular nation states that, without religious guidance, are left to invent their own moral and ethical structures. When an anti-Jewish person threw a stone through a window displaying a menorah in Bozeman, Montana, local Christian leaders called all Christians to display menorahs in their windows, which resulted in a beautiful citywide example of religious solidarity

---

3. Radhakrishnan, *Eastern Religions and Western Thought*, 2.

4. See Eck, *A New Religious America*.

5. Fredericks, *Buddhists and Christians*, xi.

in the face of hatred. And why should Christians not honor the traditions of Judaism? Was not Jesus a Jew?

But is solidarity the final aim of "interreligious dialogue"? I believe it is not; the discovery of truth is the final aim of interreligious dialogue. Solidarity results from our shared religious commitments to charity and the common good of humanity, not merely from religious dialogue. Even the Jesuit, Karl Rhaner, SJ, the go-to theologian for those who herald a new era of interreligious sameness, lucidly acknowledged that the Christian faith poses a particular problem to modern notions of "religious pluralism." He noted that such a religious pluralism:

> is a greater threat and reason for greater unrest for Christianity than for any other religion. For no other religion—not even Islam—maintains so absolutely that it is *the* religion, the one and only valid revelation of the one living God, as does the Christian religion. The fact of the pluralism of religions . . . must therefore be the greatest scandal and greatest vexation for Christianity.[6]

Given this astute view the Church's relationship with non-Christian religions and non-Catholic Christians has admittedly had moments of tension, but human behavior in times of disagreement does not change what is true. When Jesus said, "I am the way, the truth, and the life"; he went on to say that, "no one comes to the Father but by me" (John 14:6).

Whether in dialogue with other religions or in dialogue with other Christians, Christ's statement of himself cannot be set aside or relativized without disrespect to God. On the other hand, there are examples in Scripture of God's esteem for non-Christians of good heart. In the Acts of the Apostles we see Saint Peter referring to people of other faiths: "I now see how true it is that God has no favorites," he asserts, "but that in every nation, the man who is god fearing and does what is right is acceptable to him" (Acts 10:34–35). After a trip to India in 1986, Pope John Paul II issued his encyclical letter, *Dominum et vivificantem,* "The Lord, the Giver of Life," wherein the Pope recognized that the Holy Spirit is, "at the very source of the human person's existential and religious questioning."[7] He stated that, "the Holy Spirit offers to all the possibility of being associated, in a way known to God, with the Paschal Mystery."[8] In other words, spiritual inquiry, if it is genuine, points in a certain sense, with the guidance of the Holy

6. Rhaner, "Christianity and the Non-Christian Religions," 116.

7. John Paul II, *Dominum et vivificantem,* 28.

8. Ibid., 53.

Spirit, to God, offering "the possibility" of being associated with Christ. Cardinal Jean Daniélou, SJ, perhaps best expressed the Catholic position regarding non-Christian religions in his work, *The Salvation of the Nations*:

> The essential difference between Catholicism and all other religions is that the others start from man. They are touching and often very beautiful attempts, rising very high in their search for God. But in Catholicism there is a contrary movement, the descent of God towards the world, in order to communicate his life to it.[9]

The Catholic regard for other religions may be high, but the Church nonetheless calls them to final fulfillment in Jesus Christ.

Truthful dialogue between Catholics and Buddhists requires both sides of the discussion to admit areas of disagreement that are difficult to overcome, such as the seemingly impassable difference of opinions Christians and Buddhists have regarding the nature of substance, or *things* as the human mind perceives them. Buddhism, especially Theravada Buddhism, denies the reality of substance; more precisely, most Buddhists insist that *things* neither exist nor do not exist, since there is nothing "there" to define as "there" or "not there." This is an extremely important point of reference in Christian-Buddhist dialogue because Christianity adamantly insists on the existence of substance, for God has created the things we see around us. Borrowing heavily from pre-Christian Greek philosophers, Christianity employs the term *ousia*, sometimes defined as "essence," as its cornerstone for philosophical and theological inquiry. For Christians, that there are *things* there, about which we can know and discuss, is an *a priori* point from which all other discussion proceeds. Put another way, if Buddhists insist that there is no such thing as *ousia*, then dialogue has largely come to a standstill. This reminds us of medieval China, when emperors would invite Buddhists and Confucians to debate before the throne. The Buddhists would quite often begin with the complaint that Confucians were deluded by their insistence that there are *things* to discuss. To which the Confucians sardonically responded: Since Buddhists have chosen to ignore what is real, they cannot speak authoritatively about reality. These are two different worldviews that, at least in China, were never able find agreement.

---

9. Daniélou, *Salvation of the Nations*, 8.

A Note to Theologians

Regarding Christianity and other religions, such as Buddhism, I would like to add my voice to the ongoing dialogue between theologians. The reader will notice that I have read and quoted from a large number of Buddhist and Christian thinkers, many of whom identify themselves as Catholic theologians. Some of these theologians, if they have read this book, may have by now identified my theological position as somewhat "medieval," or even "harmful" to recent theological efforts to construct a new, and more "open" or "progressive" theology of religions; they may believe that I have pushed the Christian understanding of such religions as Buddhism back to a "less inclusive" era. My response to these theologians is that I have done nothing more or less than remain faithful to Catholic Christian belief and doctrine, which is itself faithful to the teachings of Jesus Christ. The goal is not to define Catholics as the "enemies" of Buddhism or any other religion for that matter; the goal is to define, and perhaps defend, Catholic belief as it compares to Buddhism, because, as Jesus said, "If you hold to my teaching, you are really my disciples. Then you will know the truth, and the truth will set you free" (John 8:31). Catholicism asserts that true liberation does not derive from *nirvana*, but from faith in Jesus Christ and membership in the Christian Church.

I have often quoted Father James Fredericks, a theologian for the Jesuit Loyola Marymount University in Los Angeles, who I often find to provide insightful and judicious comparisons between Buddhism and Christianity, but with whom I often disagree. In his chapter, "The Catholic Church and Other Religions," Fredericks outlines several categories of theological response to non-Christian religions, positions posed by, for example, Jean Daniélou, SJ, Karl Rhaner, SJ, and the extreme pluralistic ideas of John Hick; I agree most with Daniélou.

Daniélou's view of non-Christian religions such as Buddhism holds that they "find their ultimate fulfillment in Christ"; these religions "start from man," and reach, perhaps even unknowably, for God, whereas Catholicism starts with God, who has descended "toward the world" and established his Church.[10] Rhaner, on the other hand, moves beyond Daniélou's suggestion that non-Christian religions are natural expressions of the human desire for spiritual understanding; rather, for him these non-Christian

---

10. See Fredricks, *Buddhists and Christians*, 3; and Daniélou, *Salvation of the Nations*, 8.

religions function as their own, independent avenues for God's grace; Christianity need not enter into the equation. In a more radical turn away from what Jesus taught, Hick envisions a pluralistic view of religious belief. Simply stated, Hick's understanding of pluralism rejects the Christian claim that Jesus Christ is the one and only way to salvation. This pluralist assertion is that, as James Fredericks describes it, "All religions are of equal value as separate paths to salvation. Christ is but one way to this salvation."[11] The obvious question here is how Jesus, who says he is the only way to salvation, can be only one of many equal paths? If this pluralist argument is taken, then Jesus Christ would be duplicitous, which would make him a rather dubious "path to salvation."

Cardinal Jean Daniélou's theology of other religions was very influential at the Second Vatican Council precisely because it offers a way to view religious traditions such as Buddhism, that "reflect a ray of that Truth," truth which is Jesus Christ, while not compromising the eternal truths of the Christian faith. Theologians such as James Fredericks, disparage the ideas of Daniélou for holding to an outmoded Christian theology, one that I argue is most authentically the Christian one. Fredericks contends that theological views that hold Jesus Christ to be the only true path toward salvation, "have the unwelcome effect of cutting Christians off from the transformative power of the other religious traditions and their unfamiliar teachings."[12] He continues to reproach the Council's idea that other religions find fulfillment only in the Holy Spirit, suggesting rather that, "Christians should expect to find hidden within other religious traditions the same saving grace that they find in their own community."[13]

There are some theologians, too, who still hold to the phrase, "Error has its rights," which was rejected by the Council Fathers who discussed the theological insights expressed in *Nostra Aetate*. The Church's consensus regarding this phrase may be simply summarized in this way: right = correct; error = incorrect; thus, error ≠ right. A person might have freedom to choose error, but error itself has no rights because it is not, so to speak, right. Catholic Christianity may have theological mystery, but even mystery must be checked against reason. And when theologians jettison reason and formulate new theological paradigms in order to create "interreligious solidarity," they are in danger of Relativism, which is a distortion of truth and

11. Fredricks, *Buddhists and Christians*, 6.

12. Ibid., 18.

13. Ibid., 18.

is philosophically indefensible. An example: in his criticism of the traditional Catholic theology regarding non-Christian religions, which he calls "fulfillment theology," James Fredericks condemns the Catholic view that, "Buddhist compassion ... [is actually] a sign of the Holy Spirit because it is analogous to Christian love."[14] Rather, Fredericks recommends that Christians take seriously the Buddhist call to, "renounce their belief in God as an unhelpful entanglement that does not lead to liberation from suffering," for, after all, "Error has its rights."[15] Such Buddhist challenges to Christian belief, Fredericks continues, are opportunities for "self-enrichment."[16] The Church disagrees, and calls such positions Relativism.

In his General Audience on 17 October 2012, Pope Benedict XVI reminded the faithful of the hazards of such intellectual views:

> Relativism leads, on the contrary, to having no reference points, suspicion and volubility break up human relations, while life is lived in brief experiments without the assumption of responsibility. If individualism and relativism seem to dominate the minds of many of our contemporaries, it cannot be said that believers are completely immune to these dangers, with which we are confronted in the transmission of the faith.[17]

Christians admit, as Pope Benedict XVI has said, that "the mystery of God always remains beyond our conception and reason," but unlike other traditions, such as Buddhism, in Christianity "through his revelation, God actually communicates himself to us, recounts himself and makes himself accessible."[18] We are not alone to imagine, to grope, for truth; God has revealed himself to humanity in his Word and in his Church. As Saint Paul wrote: "I preached to you the Gospel, which you received, in which you stand, by which you are saved, if you hold it fast—unless you believed in vain" (1 Cor 15:2).

14. Ibid., 19.
15. Ibid.
16. Ibid.
17. Benedict XVI, General Audience.
18. Ibid.

Buddhism, God, and the Waters of Truth

Shortly before Pope John Paul II's visit to St. Patrick's Cathedral in 1979, when the Dalai Lama was greeted there, a monsignor in the receiving line recounted his short meeting with the Buddhist patriarch. The Dalai Lama approached him and asked him very directly, "Father, do you know the difference between you and me?" "No, Your Holiness," answered the monsignor. "You believe in a personal God," the Dalai Lama declared, "and I do not." In this passing dialogue the Dalai Lama was telling the truth; beyond the important and admirable rhetoric of peace, compassion, and religious solidarity, there remains an authentic difference between Jesus and Buddha: Jesus is God; Buddha is not.

Despite our differences and despite some social pressures to accept "all truths as equally valid," I remain convinced that Buddhists and Christians can, and must, become friends, friends who better understand one another without compromising the truth. Yet, as Christians we continue to recall an important command of the Our Father, "Thy will be done on earth as it is in heaven," and we remain obedient to the teachings of Christ, who said, "You are my friends if you do what I command" (John 15:14). The fact that God has become Man, has reached out to us, and has suffered for us is always present in our minds; and God's gift extends to all. During his anguish in the Garden of Gethsemane, Jesus demonstrated authentic liberation, which is surrender to the personal God who is waiting to be fully known by those who do not yet believe in him. During his agony, Jesus said to his Father, "Not as I will, but as you will"; this is, according to Christian belief, genuine freedom (Matt 26:39). And as Cardinal Joseph Ratzinger said in his homily on April 18, 2005, shortly before his election to pope, "Truly, the love and friendship of God was given to us so that it might also be shared with others."[19]

In a final word to other Christians who feel disheartened by the apparent failure of their dialogue with Buddhists; we must keep in mind that Christian witness often grows slowly from the seeds one plants. C. S. Lewis, himself a convert, once said that, "The very man who has argued you down, will sometimes be found, years later, to have been influenced by what you said."[20] And this brings us to something else C. S. Lewis said, or rather,

19. Ratzinger, "Homily of His Eminence, Cardinal Joseph Ratzinger, Dean of the College of Cardinals."

20. Lewis, *Reflections on the Psalms*, 73.

something that Aslan said. In his novel, *The Silver Chair*, which is part of the beautifully written Chronicles of Narnia, there is a passage wherein Jill Pole, a young English schoolgirl, finds herself unexpectedly in Aslan's country. After waking up in this curious place she is struck with a sudden thirst, and follows the sound of running water to "an open glade and saw the stream, bright as glass, running across the turf a stone's throw away from her." But Jill was too frightened to approach the water, despite her growing thirst, for "just on the side of the stream lay the lion." "If you're thirsty, you may drink," said the lion. And then again, the lion said, "If you are thirsty, come and drink." Paralyzed with fear, the girl still refused to approach the stream. "I'm *dying* of thirst," said Jill. "Then drink, "said the lion. "I daren't come and drink," said Jill. "Then you will die of thirst," said the lion.

But Jill still refused to step nearer the water. "I suppose I must go and look for another stream then." To which, the lion answered, "There is no other stream."[21]

---

21. Lewis, *Chronicles of Narnia*, 557–58.

The Creed Compared

In response to attempts to define Christianity and Buddhism as "two paths to the same end," I have provided here a comparison of the two religions based on the Christian Nicene Creed. More complete explanations of these differences are found in the main part of this book, but this brief section will serve to highlight the essential distinctions between the Christian and Buddhist "paths." One will notice that the centerpiece that holds Christianity distinct from Buddhism is the enduring Christian belief in God, who is the creator and redeemer of all human persons. Nearly every creedal difference between Christians and Buddhists relates in some significant way to this belief.

I believe in one God, the Father, the Almighty. . . .

For Buddhists there is no "I," or self, to believe in, just as there is no "God" to believe in.

. . . . maker of heaven and earth,
of all that is seen and unseen.

Buddhism accepts neither the existence of a creator nor a creation, and it rejects dichotomies such as "heaven" and "earth"; and finally, what is "seen and unseen" is held to be an illusion.

I believe in one Lord, Jesus Christ,
the only Son of God. . . .

Faith in an external "God" is not intrinsic to Buddhism, and Jesus Christ,
according to many Buddhists is considered to be a holy teacher.

. . . . eternally begotten of the Father, God from God,
Light from Light, true God from true God, begotten,
not made, one in being with the Father.

Buddhism has no concept of consubstantiality or trinitarianism; since Buddhists largely reject belief in God as an obstacle to *nirvana*, the Christian
definition of the Trinity is impractical.

Through Him all things were made.

Again, creation is rejected from the Buddhist point of view, and is replaced
by the notion of an eternal regression. According to Buddhists, there was
no creation, but rather, the cosmos has always existed.

For us men and our salvation He came down from
heaven.

The Buddhist notion of "salvation" is very unlike the Christian one; the
Buddhist idea of "salvation" is *nirvana*, or the extinction of the self and the
liberation from rebirth.

By the power of the Holy Spirit, He was born of the
Virgin Mary, and became man.

These concepts are uniquely Christian and have no counterparts in Buddhism; while there might be some parallels between Mary's virginal birth of
Jesus and the legendary birth of the Buddha, the Christian understanding
of Christ's Incarnation is absent from Buddhist belief.

For our sake He was crucified under Pontius Pilate; He suffered, died, and was buried.

Redemptive suffering is unimagined in Buddhism; Buddhism believes that death can only result in either rebirth or *moksha* (liberation from rebirth) in the next life. As there is no creator-god in Buddhism, there is none to pay for sins.

On the third day He rose again in fulfillment of the scriptures.

Buddhists do not accept Christian Scripture as "revealed from God," and thus prophecy and fulfillment in non-Buddhist canons are not relevant to the Buddhist goal of liberation from suffering.

He ascended into heaven and is seated at the right hand of the Father.

Many Buddhists hold that Christ's Ascension is part of the Christian imagination, and thus find no use for the Christian belief in the Father and the Son's co-divinity.

He will come again in glory to judge the living and the dead, and his kingdom will have no end.

Some forms of Buddhism might speak of beings that are judged, but both the judged and the judges, not being God, are themselves subject to rebirth and subsequent judgment. As there is no God according to Buddhism, there can thus be no "kingdom" of God. Finally, the Buddhist doctrine of impermanence differently imagines the existential reality of beginnings and endings.

We believe in the Holy Spirit, the Lord, the giver of life, who proceeds from the Father (and the Son).

Trinitarian theology is problematic for Buddhists since Buddhism has no theology, as theology, being the study (-*ology*) of God (*theo-*) is irrelevant to Buddhism, which does not consider the existence of a creator God.

With the Father and the Son, He is worshiped and glorified.

With no concept of a Holy Spirit, in the Christian sense, Buddhism cannot "worship and glorify" what it does not believe to exist.

He has spoken through the Prophets.

Buddhism recognizes no "prophets" from the Old Testament, nor does it recognize the presence of a God to "speak through" them.

We believe in one, holy, catholic, and apostolic Church.

Whereas Catholic Christians recognize "one, holy, catholic, and apostolic Church," which is based on Jesus Christ, who is God, Buddhists naturally do not follow this belief, as they do not believe in God. Buddhists, in contrast, commit themselves to the Buddhist samgha, or community, along with the Buddha and the *dharma*.

We acknowledge one baptism for the forgiveness of sins.

Baptism is irrelevant to Buddhists who do not share the Christian understanding of the Fall or sin, which is a violation of God's will. Indeed, according to Buddhism there is no God whose will can be violated.

We look for the resurrection of the dead, and the life of the world to come.

According to Catholics, there will be a "general resurrection," when the souls of all persons will rise again with their bodies, and those who have been judged worthy will enter into what is called the "Beatific Vision," which is when a person enters into perfect salvation in God's presence as a member of the communion of saints. Buddhism, however, views the persistence of the human body as an illusory "self," which is in a state of continual suffering. The Buddhist goal is to attain *nirvana*, a state of neither being nor non-being, which is contrary to the Christian understanding of a permanent soul, a resurrected body, and an afterlife. Saint Thomas More perhaps best answered the Buddhist belief that all human existence is suffering when he said, "Earth has no sorrow that Heaven cannot heal."[1]

1. More, "Come, Ye Disconsolate," in *The Cambridge Book of Poetry and Song,* 387.

Bibliography

Alen, George Francis. *The Buddha's Philosophy: Selections from the Pali Canon and an Introductory Essay.* New York: Macmillan, 1959.

Anselm. *Basic Writings.* Translated by Sidney Norton. Grand Rapids: Christian Classics Ethereal Library, 1903.

Aquinas, Thomas. *Summa Theologicae.* New York: Benziger Brothers, 1947.

Archimandrite Sophrony. *His Life is Mine.* Translated by Rosemary Edmonds. Crestwood, NY: St. Vladimir's Seminary Press, 1977.

Aronson, Harvey. "Buddhist Practice in Relation to Self-Representation: A Cross-Cultural Dialogue." In *Buddhism and Psychotherapy Across Cultures,* edited by Mark Unno, 61–85. Boston: Wisdom Publications, 2006.

Augustine. *The Confessions of St. Augustine.* Translated by Rex Warner. New York: New American Library, 1963.

Barragán, Cardinal Javier Lozano. "A Christian Understanding of Pain and Suffering." *L'Osservatore Romano,* September 7, 2005.

Benedict XVI., Pope. "Post-Synodal Apostolic Exhortation," *Verbum Domini,* September 30, 2010.

———. *Caritas in Veritate.*

———. *Deus Caritas Est.*

———. General Audience, October 17, 2012.

Berry, T. Sterling. *Christianity and Buddhism: A Comparison and Contrast.* London: Society for Promoting Christian Knowledge, 1890.

Berry, Thomas. *Buddhism.* New York: Hawthorn Books, 1967.

Bhikkhu Bodhi. *The Middle Length Discourses of the Buddha: A Translation of the Majjhima Nikaya.* Translated by Bhikkhu Nanamoli. Boston: Wisdom, 1995.

Bielefeldt, Carl. *Dogen's Manuals of Zen Meditation.* Berkeley: University of California Press, 1988.

Bohr, David. *Catholic Moral Tradition.* Huntington, IN: Our Sunday Visitor, 1999.

Boniface III, Pope. *Unam Sanctam,* November 18, 1302.

Bourgeault, Cynthia. *Centering Prayer and Inner Awakening.* Lanham, MD: Cowley, 2004.

Bowen, Anthony, and Peter Garnsey, trans. *Lactantius, Divine Institutes.* Liverpool: Liverpool University Press, 2003.

Brewster, E. H. *The Life of Gotama the Buddha*. London: Kegan Paul, Trench, Trubner, 1926

Buddhadasa Bhikkhu. *Handbook for Mankind*. Tullera, Australia: Buddha Dharma Education Association, 1996.

Buri, Fritz. "A Comparison of Buddhism and Christianity According to a History of Problems." In *Buddhist-Christian Dialogue: Mutual Renewal and Transformation*, edited by Paul O. Ingram and Frederick J. Streng, 15–33. Honolulu: University of Hawaii Press, 1986.

Cabezón, José Ignacio. "Three Buddhist Views of the Doctrines of Creation and Creator." In *Buddhism, Christianity and the Question of Creation: Karmic or Divine?*, edited by Perry Scmidt-Leukel. Aldershot, England: Ashgate, 2006. Kindle.

———, ed. *Buddhism, Sexuality, and Gender*. New York: SUNY, 1992.

Catechism of the Catholic Church: With modifications from the Editio Typica. New York: Doubleday, 2003.

Ch'en, Kenneth K. S. *Buddhism: The Light of Asia*. Woodbury, NY: Barron's Educational Series, 1968.

Chesterton, G. K. "Buddhism and Christianity." *Illustrated London News*, March 2, 1929.

———. *What's Wrong with the World?* New York: Dodd, Mead, and Co., 1912.

Christian Discussion Forum. "Buddha vs. Jesus." Part 1. http://www.webring.org.

Compendium of the History of the Cistercian Order. Gethsemani, KY: Order of Cistercians of the Strict Observance, 1944.

Congregation for the Doctrine of Faith. "Instruction on Respect for Human Life in its Origin and the Dignity of Procreation." February 22, 1987.

Conze, Edward, ed., et al. *Buddhist Texts Through the Ages*. New York: Harper Torchbooks, 1954.

———. *Buddhism: Its Essence and Development*. New York: Harper Torchbooks, 1959.

Cunningham, Eric. *Zen Past and Present*. Ann Arbor, MI: Association for Asian Studies, 2011.

Dalai Lama. *Freedom in Exile: The Autobiography of the Dalai Lama*. New York: Cornelia & Michael Bessie, 1990.

———. "The Dalai Lama." Interview by Claudia Dreifus. *New York Times*, November 28, 1993.

———. *Stages of Meditation*. Translated by Geshe Lobsang Jordhen and Jeremy Russell. Ithaca, NY: Snow Lion, 2001.

———. *The Dalai Lama at Harvard*. Translated by Jeffrey Hopkins. Ithaca: Snow Lion, 1988.

———. *The Good Heart: A Buddhist Perspective on the Teachings of Jesus*. Summerville, MA: Wisdom Publications, 1996.

Daniel-Rops, Henri. *What is the Bible?* Translated by J. R. Foster. New York: Hawthorn, 1958.

Daniélou, Jean, SJ. *The Salvation of the Nations*. Notre Dame, IN: University of Notre Dame Press, 1962.

Davids, Caroline A. F. Rhys, ed. *Stories of the Buddha: Being Selections from the Jataka*. New York: Dover, 1989.

Dolan, Cardinal Timothy. "Archbishop Dolan Defines Human Dignity as 'Primary Doctrine' of Church." *Catholic News Service*, December 7, 2011.

Dreher, John D. "The Danger of Centering Prayer." *This Rock* 8 (November 1997) 14–16.

Drinan, Robert, SJ. "A Zen Retreat," Accessed February 28, 2013. http://kennedyzen. tripod.com/retreat_drinan.htm.

Duffy, Regis, OFM, and Angelus Gambatese, OFM, eds. *Made in God's Image: The Catholic Vision of Human Dignity.* New York: Paulist, 1999.

Dumoulin, Heinrich. *The Development of Chinese Zen after the Sixth Patriarch.* Taipei: SMC, 1953

Dunne, Carrin. *Buddha and Jesus: Conversations.* Springfield, IL: Templegate, 1975.

Dutt, Manmatha Nath. *Buddha: His Life, His Teachings, His Order.* Calcutta: Society for the Resuscitation of Indian Literature, 1901.

Dynes, Wayne R., and Stephen Donaldson, eds. *Asian Homosexuality.* New York: Garland, 1992.

Eck, Diana. *A New Religious America: How a "Christian Country" Has Become the World's Most Religiously Diverse Nation.* San Francisco: HarperSanFrancisco, 2001.

Flott, Anthony. "When Worlds that Should Collide, Don't." *National Catholic Register,* June 5, 2007.

Fox, Thomas C. "Double Belonging: Buddhism and Christian faith," *National Catholic Reporter.* June 23, 2010.

Fredericks, James L. *Buddhists and Christians: Through Comparative Theology to Solidarity.* Maryknoll, NY: Orbis, 2004.

Graham, Dom Aelred. *Zen Catholicism.* New York: Crossroad, 1963.

Gregory, Peter N. ed. *Traditions of Meditation in Chinese Buddhism.* Honolulu: University of Hawaii Press, 1986.

Guang Xing. *The Concept of the Buddha: Its Evolution from Early Buddhism to Trikaya Theory.* New York: Routledge, 2005.

Gupta, S. K. *Elephant in Indian Art and Mythology.* New Delhi: Abhinav Publications, 1990.

Harris, T. George. "The Peaceful Mind: An Interview with His Holiness the Dalai Lama," http://www.beliefnet.com/faiths/buddhism/2000/05/the-peaceful-mind.aspx.

Harvey, Peter. *An Introduction to Buddhism: Teachings, History and Practices.* Cambridge: Cambridge University Press, 1990.

————. *Introduction to Buddhist Ethics.* Cambridge: Cambridge University Press, 2000.

Heng Sure. "Pope Benedict XVI's Buddhist Encounter," *Dharma Forest,* April 20, 2005. http://paramita.typepad.com/dharma_forest/2005/04/pope_benedict_x.html.

Henry, Patrick ed. *Benedict's Dharma: Buddhist Reflections on the Rule of Saint Benedict.* New York: Riverhead, 2001.

Herbermann, Charles G., ed., et al. *The Catholic Encyclopedia.* New York: Robert Appleton, 1908.

————. *The Catholic Encyclopedia: An International Work of Reference on the Constitution, Doctrine, Discipline, and History of the Catholic Church.* New York: The Encyclopedia Press, 1913.

Hisao Inagaki. *The Three Pure Land Sutras: A Study and Translation from Chinese.* Kyoto: Nagata Bunshodo, 1994.

Hsing Yun. *Humanistic Buddhism: A Blueprint for Life.* Translated by John Balcom. Hacienda Heights, CA: Buddha's Light, 2008.

Hunter, Sylvester Joseph. *Outlines of Dogmatic Theology.* New York: Benziger Brothers, 1895.

Ingram, Paul O., and Frederick J. Streng, eds. *Buddhist-Christian Dialogue: Mutual Renewal and Transformation.* Honolulu: University of Hawaii Press, 1986.

International Theological Commission. "Select Questions on the Theology of the Redeemer." October 7, 1995.

Jackson, Peter A. "Male Homosexuality and Transgenderism in the Thai Buddhist Tradition." http://buddhism.lib.ntu.edu.tw/museum/TAIWAN/md/md08-52.htm.

Jefford, Clayton N., ed. *The Didache in Context: Essays on its Text, History, & Transmission.* Leiden: Brill, 1995.

Jeffrey, David Lyle. *Luke.* Brazos Theological Commentary on the Bible. Grand Rapids: Brazos, 2012.

John XIII, Pope. *Ad Petri Cathedram.* Encyclical on Truth, Unity, and Peace, in a Spirit of Charity. June 29, 1959.

―――. *Pacem in Terris.* Encyclical on Establishing Universal Peace in Truth, Justice, Peace and Liberty. April 11, 1963.

John Paul II, Pope. "Address to Representatives of Buddhism and Shinto in Japan," February 20, 1980.

―――. "Message for the XXVII World Day of Peace," January 1, 1994.

―――. *Crossing the Threshold of Hope.* New York: Knopf, 1995.

―――. *Dominum et vivificantem.*

―――. *Evangelium Vitae.*

―――. Pentecost Homily, May 30, 1998.

―――. *Redemptoris Missio.*

―――. *Redemtoris Missio.*

―――. *Salvifici Doloris.*

―――. *Sollicitudo Rei Socialis.*

―――. *Tertio Millenio Adveniente*

Keating, Thomas. "Foreword." In Cynthia Bourgeault, *Centering Prayer and Inner Awakening,* vi-viii. Lanham, MD: Cowley, 2004.

―――. *Intimacy with God.* New York: Crossroad, 1994.

à Kempis, Thomas. *My Imitation of Christ.* Brooklyn: Confraternity of the Precious Blood, 1954.

Kennedy, Robert E. *Zen Spirit, Christian Spirit: The Place of Zen in Christian Life.* New York: Continuum, 1997.

Kern, H., trans. *The Saddharma-Pundarīka or The Lotus of the True-law.* Sacred Books of the East 21. Oxford: Clarendon, 1909.

Kerouac, Jack. *The Dharma Bums.* New York: Penguin, 1958.

Knitter, Paul F. *Without Buddha I Could Not Be a Christian.* London: Oneworld, 2009.

Kornfield, Jack. "Introduction." In Marcus Borg, *Jesus and Buddha: The Parallel Sayings,* i-iii. Berkeley: Ulysses, 1997.

Kreeft, Peter. *Making Sense Out of Suffering.* Ann Arbor, MI: Servant, 1986.

Lattin, Don. "Dalai Lama Speaks on Gay Sex." *San Francisco Chronicle,* June 11, 1997.

Lefebure, Leo D. *The Buddha and the Christ: Explorations in Buddhist and Christian Dialogue.* New York: Maryknoll, 1993.

Leo XIII, Pope. *Providentissimus Deus.*

Lewis, C. S. *Reflections on the Psalms.* San Diego: Harvest, 1986.

―――. *The Chronicles of Narnia.* New York: HarperCollins, 1998.

Li Tiangang. "Father Malatesta and the Chinese Scholars." In *Edward Malatesta, SJ: A Friend of China,* edited by James S. Torrens. St. Louis, MO: Institute of Jesuit Sources, 2004.

Lumen gentium, the Dogmatic Constitution on the Church. Documents of the Second Vatican Council. November 21, 1964.

Magliola, Robert. *Facing Up to Real Doctrinal Difference: How Some Thought-Motifs from Derrida can Nourish the Catholic-Buddhist Encounter.* Kettering, OH: Angelico, 2014.

Mair, Victor H., trans. *Wandering on the Way: Early Taoist Tales and Parables of Chuang Tzu.* New York: Bantam, 1994.

Majjhimanikaya Sutra, no. 72. https://www.dhammatalks.org/suttas/MN/index_MN.html.

de Mello, Anthony, SJ. *Sadhana: A Way to God; Christian Exercises in Eastern Form.* St. Louis, MO: The Insitute of Jesuit Sources, 1987.

Merton, Thomas. *Mystics & Zen Masters.* New York: Dell, 1961.

———. *The Asian Journals of Thomas Merton.* New York: New Directions, 1968.

———. *The Living Bread.* New York: Farrar, Straus, and Cudahy, 1956.

———. *Zen and the Birds of Appetite.* New York: New Directions, 1968.

———. *The Seven Story Mountain.* New York: Harcourt, Brace, 1948.

Mikio Matsuoka. "The Buddhist Concept of the Human Being: From the Viewpoint of the Philosophy of the Soka Gakkai." *The Journal of Oriental Studies* 15 (2005) 51.

More, Thomas. "Come, Ye Disconsolate." In *The Cambridge Book of Poetry and Song,* edited by Charlotte Fiske Bates, 387. New York: Thomas Y. Crowell, 1882.

Moskowitz, Marc L. *The Haunting Fetus: Abortion, Sexuality, and the Spirit World in Taiwan.* Honolulu: University of Hawaii Press, 2001.

Mote, Frederick W. *Intellectual Foundations of China.* New York: Knopf, 1971.

Mother Teresa, National Prayer Breakfast in Washington, DC, February 5, 1994. http://www.john654.org/MotherTPrayerBreakfast.html.

Müller, Friedrich M. *Wisdom of the Buddha: The Unabridged Dhammapada.* New York: Cosimo, 2007.

Murray, Charles B. *Prosperity of the Soul: The Evolution of Man.* Bloomington, IN: AuthorHouse, 2008.

Naquin, Susan, and Chun-fang Yu. *Pilgrims and Sacred Sites in China.* Berkeley: University of California Press, 1992.

Narada Mahathera. *The Buddha and His Teachings.* Mumbai: Jaico, 2006.

Nattier, Jan. "The Meanings of the Maitreya Myth." In *Maitreya, The Future Buddha,* edited by Alan Sponberg and Helen Hardacre, 23–47. Cambridge: Cambridge University Press, 1988.

The New Catholic Encyclopedia. New York: Universal Knowledge Foundation, 1929.

Partner, Daniel. *Quicknotes: Great Women of Faith.* Carol Stream, IL: Tyndale House, 2000.

Paul VI, Pope. "Address to Representatives of Japanese Buddhism," November 7, 1966.

———. *Apostolic Exhortation Evangelii Nuntiandi.*

———. *Dei Verbum.* November 18, 1965.

———. *Nostra Aetate.* October 28, 1965

Percheron, Maurice. *Buddha and Buddhism.* New York: Harper, 1960.

Pieper, Josef. *Abuse of Language, Abuse of Power.* San Francisco: Ignatius, 1992.

Pius XI, Pope. *Casti Connubii.*

Plato. *Dialogues of Plato.* Translated by Benjamin Jowett. Cambridge: Cambridge University Press, 1871, 2010.

———. *The Works of Plato.* Edited by Edwin Irwin. New York: The Modern Library, 1956.

BIBLIOGRAPHY

"Pope Benedict XVI Promotes Biblical Meditation." *Zenit*, September 16, 2005. https://zenit.org/articles/benedict-xvi-promotes-biblical-meditation/.

Posnov, Mikhail, and Thomas E. Herman. *The History of the Christian Church Until the Great Schism of 1054*. Bloomington, IN: AuthorHouse, 2004.

Price, A. F. and Wong Mou-lam, trans. *The Diamond Sutra & the Sutra of Hui-neng*. Boston: Shambala, 1990.

Price, Charlie. *50 Questions on the Natural Law: What It is and Why We Need It*. San Francisco: Ignatius, 1999.

Radhakrishnan, S. *Eastern Religions and Western Thought*. New York: Oxford University Press, 1959.

Ratzinger, Cardinal Joseph. *Declaration. "Dominus Iesus" On the Unicity and Salvific Universality of Jesus Christ And The Church*. August 6, 2000.

————. *Letter to the Bishops of the Catholic Church on Some Aspects of Christian Meditation*. Congregation for the Doctrine of the Faith. October 15, 1989.

————. *Homily of His Eminence Card. Joseph Ratzinger, Dean of the College of Cardinals*. April 18, 2005.

Rhaner, Karl, SJ. "Christianity and the Non-Christian Religions." In *Theological Investigations*, Volume 5, 115–34. Baltimore: Helicon, 1966.

Rhodes, M. J. *The Visible Unity of the Catholic Church*. Volume 1. London: Longmans, Green, 1870.

Ricci, Matteo, SJ. *The True Meaning of the Lord of Heaven* (T'ien-chu Shih-i). Translated by Douglas Lancashire and Peter Hu Kuo-chen, SJ. Taipei: Ricci Institute, 1985.

Robinson, Richard H., et al. *Buddhist Religions: A Historical Introduction*. Fifth Edition. Belmont, CA: Thomson Wadsworth, 2005.

Rolheiser, Ronald. *The Holy Longing: The Search for a Christian Spirituality*. New York: Doubleday, 1999.

Scmidt-Leukel, Perry, ed. *Buddhism, Christianity and the Question of Creation: Karmic or Divine?* Aldershot, England: Ashgate, 2006.

Scullion, James P., OFM. "Creation-Incarnation: God's Affirmation of Human Worth." In *Made in God's Image: The Catholic Vision of Human Dignity*, edited by Regis Duffy, OFM, and Angelus Gambatese, OFM, 7–15. New York: Paulist, 1999.

Seichi Yagi. "Paul and Shinren; Jesus and Zen: What Lies at the Ground of Human Existence?" In *Buddhist-Christian Dialogue: Mutual Renewal and Transformation*, edited by Paul O. Ingram, 197–216. Eugene, OR: Wipf & Stock, 2007.

Shantideva and Padmakara Translation Group. *The Way of the Bodhisattva*. Boston: Shambhala, 2006.

Siegmund, Georg. *Buddhism and Christianity: A Preface to Dialogue*. Translated by Sr Mary Francis McCarthy. Tuscaloosa: The University of Alabama Press, 1980.

Soothill, W. E. *The Lotus of the Wonderful Way: Or the Lotus Gospel*. London: Curzon Press, 1987.

Sponberg, Alan, and Helen Hardacre, eds. *Maitreya, The Future Buddha*. Cambridge: Cambridge University Press, 1988.

Stabile, Susan J. "A Christian Faith Enriched by Buddhism," *Huffington Post*, November 13, 2012.

————. *Growing in Love and Wisdom: Tibetan Buddhist Sources for Christian Meditation*. Oxford: Oxford University Press, 2013.

Strong, John S. *The Experience of Buddhism: Sources and Interpretations*. Third edition. Belmont, CA: Thomson Wadsworth, 2008.

Stryk, Lucien, ed. *World of the Buddha: An Introduction to Buddhist Literature.* Garden City, NY: Doubleday, 1968.

Surya Das (Jeffrey Miller). *Awakening the Buddha Within: Tibetan Wisdom for the Western World.* New York: Broadway, 1998.

Suzuki, D. T. *An Introduction to Zen Buddhism.* New York: Grove, 1964.

———. *The Lankavatara Sutra: A Mahayana Text.* Reprint. Taipei: SMC, 1994.

———. *Mysticism: Christian and Buddhist.* New York: Macmillan, 1957.

———. *Outlines of Mahayana Buddhism.* New York: Schocken, 1963.

———. *Studies in Zen.* London: Rider, 1955.

Taye, Jamgon. *Enthronement: The Recognition of the Reincarnate Masters of Tibet and the Himalayas.* Translated by Ngawang Zangpo. Ithaca, NY: Snow Lion, 1997.

Thanissaro Bikkhu (Geoffrey Degraff). *Handful of Leaves: Volume Three.* Redwood City, CA: The Sati Center for Buddhist Studies, 2003.

Thich Nhat Hanh. *Going Home: Jesus and Buddha as Brothers.* New York: Riverhead, 1999.

———. *Living Buddha, Living Christ.* New York: Riverhead, 1995.

Torrens, James S., SJ, and Xiaoxin Wu, eds. *Edward Malatesta, SJ: A Friend of China.* Saint Louis: Institute of Jesuit Sources, 2004.

Trainor, Kevin, ed. *Buddhism.* Oxford: Oxford University Press, 2004.

Tsomo, Karma Lekshe. "Prolife, Prochoice: Buddhism and Reproductive Ethics." *Feminism and Nonviolence Studies* (Fall 1998). http://www.fnsa.org/fall98/fall98.html.

Tucci, Guiseppe. *The Religions of Tibet.* Translated by Geoffrey Samuel. Berkeley: University of California Press, 1980.

Tworkov, Helen. *Zen in America: Profiles of Five Teachers.* San Francisco: North Point, 1989.

Unno, Mark, ed. *Buddhism and Psychotherapy Across Cultures.* Boston: Wisdom, 2006.

Van Dyke, Henry, ed. *Little Masterpieces of English Poetry by British and American Authors.* Volume IV. New York: Doubleday, 1907.

Wallis, Glenn, trans. *The Dhammapada: Verses on the Way.* New York: The Modern Library, 2007.

Warren, Henry Clarke. *Buddhism in Translations.* New York: Atheneum, 1963.

Welch, Holmes. *The Practice of Chinese Buddhism, 1900–1950.* Cambridge: Harvard University Press, 1967.

Wu, John C. H. *The Golden Age of Zen.* Taipei: United Publishing Center, 1975.

Yampolsky, Philip B., translator. *The Platform Sutra of the Sixth Patriarch.* New York: Columbia University Press, 1967.

Yandell, Keith, and Harold Netland. *Buddhism: A Christian Exploration and Appraisal.* Downers Grove, IL: InterVarsity, 2009.

Index

Made in the USA
Lexington, KY
03 June 2018